Living by God's Promises

Deepen Your Christian Life

From the late 1500s to the early 1700s, Puritan ministers wrote thousands of Christian books that contain massive amounts of biblical, doctrinal, experiential, and practical instruction to energize and deepen your Christian life. During that period, thousands of volumes coming off English presses consisted of Puritan sermon material popularized in book form. Unfortunately, many believers today find it difficult to read the antiquarian Puritan language and, when they attempt to do so, find themselves more frustrated than energized.

This new series, Deepen Your Christian Life, presents in contemporary language the major teachings that several Puritans wrote on subjects that are seldom addressed adequately, if at all, today. Finally, you too will be able to enjoy the Puritans and experience, by the Spirit's grace, that they really do deepen your Christian life.

Living by God's Promises
    Joel R. Beeke and James La Belle (2010)

Living Zealously
    Joel R. Beeke and James La Belle (forthcoming)

Living with a Good Conscience
    Joel R. Beeke (forthcoming)

Living by God's Promises

with Study Questions

Joel R. Beeke and James A. La Belle

Foreword by Jerry Bridges

Reformation Heritage Books
Grand Rapids, Michigan

Living by God's Promises
©2010 by Joel R. Beeke and James A. La Belle

Reformation Heritage Books
2965 Leonard St., NE,
Grand Rapids, MI 49525
616-977-0889 / Fax 616-285-3246
orders@heritagebooks.org
www.heritagebooks.org

Printed in the United States of America
10 11 12 13 14 15/10 9 8 7 6 5 4 3 2 1

Library of Congress Cataloging-in-Publication Data

Beeke, Joel R., 1952-
  Living by God's promises / Joel R. Beeke and James A. La Belle.
    p. cm.
  ISBN 978-1-60178-104-8 (pbk. : alk. paper)
  1. God (Christianity)—Promises—Biblical teaching. 2. Christian life—Puritan authors. 3. Puritans—Doctrines. I. La Belle, James A. II. Title.
  BS680.P68B44 2010
  231.7— dc22
                        2010034404

For additional Reformed literature, both new and used, request a free book list from Reformation Heritage Books at the above regular or e-mail address.

Table of Contents

With heartfelt appreciation to

Michael Haykin and Derek Thomas

faithful friends and prolific authors,
fellow conference speakers and seminary colleagues,
whose minds function and hearts beat like contemporary Puritans;
in Christ,

I thank my God upon every remembrance of you (Philippians 1:3).

— JRB

⟹ ◆◆ ⟸

With heartfelt appreciation to

Chantry C. La Belle

for your unending love and encouragement,
for your faithfulness and consistency,
for your friendship and trust,
for your laughter and joy.

*Truly, in you, I have found a good thing and obtained
favor from the LORD* (Proverbs 18:22).

— JAL

Foreword

The Bible is God's self-revelation to humanity. In a broad sense, it tells us who God is, what He requires of us, and what He has promised to us. We call these last two *precepts* and *promises*.

Among Christians today, there is a tremendous amount of biblical illiteracy. Many seldom, or never, read their Bible. They attend church somewhat regularly and listen to perhaps a 25-minute motivational message that may or may not be based on Scripture. But they never read or study the Bible for themselves.

A second group of believers are more dedicated. They read their Bibles, perhaps attend an adult Sunday school class and listen to a biblically based sermon every Sunday. They have a reasonable knowledge of Scripture. But the thought of applying the Bible to their daily lives in an intentional and specific way has never occurred to them. They, to a degree, possess much factual knowledge of Scripture but pay little attention to its precepts.

There is still a third group of believers who take seriously the precepts of Scripture. They do seek to apply the Bible to their daily lives; but unfortunately, they know little about appropriating and praying over God's promises.

My perception of our Christian community is that only a small minority of believers are both seeking to obey the precepts and live by the promises of God's Word.

This is where the book, *Living by God's Promises*, can help us. It is the most thorough treatment of this subject that I have ever seen. Interestingly enough, the book is based on the writings of three Puritan pastors. The present authors —Joel Beeke and James La Belle—have attempted to make the writings of these Puritan authors more reader-friendly to twenty-first-century readers who are not used to the heavy style of seventeenth-century writers.

The Puritan pastors of the seventeenth century have suffered from a lot of erroneous "bad press" in recent years. They have, for the most part, been portrayed as uptight legalists. The truth is that they were probably more grace-centered and more warmly devotional in their relationship with God than any succeeding era of evangelical Christendom.

So, what do these Puritan pastors say about living by the promises of God? Beeke and La Belle have done an outstanding job of fleshing that out, and I will not seek to preempt them. But one thing stands out to me. These Puritan pastors believed that all the promises of God, at least in principle, are available to us today. This means there is not a single situation that arises in your life for which there is not a promise from God that will address that situation.

The Apostle Paul wrote in 2 Corinthians 1:20, "For all the promises of God in him (that is, in Christ) are yea, and in him Amen." This is true in two ways. First, Jesus at His first advent was the actual fulfillment of many of the Old Testament prophecies and will, in the future, be the fulfillment of other promises at His second coming.

Second, and important to us, His sinless life and sin-bearing death provide the meritorious basis upon which any promise is made good to us. Apart from Christ, we have no right to any of God's promises. But through our union with Christ, we have access to all of them.

The purpose of a foreword is to introduce and commend the work of the author(s). So, I must refrain from giving my own testimony to the joy I have personally experienced in living by the promises of God. I could only wish that I had been more intentional and specific about this in my earlier years as a Christian.

Joshua 21:45 says, "There failed not aught of any good thing which the LORD had spoken [literally, promised] unto the house of Israel; all came to pass." This can also be true for us as we learn from these godly Puritans how to live by the promises of God. It is to that end that I warmly commend this book to you.

—Jerry Bridges

Introduction

The first volume of the new series, "Deepen Your Christian Life," which addresses the promises of God, fulfills a longstanding dream. For many years, we envisioned a collection of Puritan material on important areas of practical Christian living that are not adequately addressed in Christian literature today. Our goal is to condense this material and contemporize its language so that each short paperback book in the series covers one important topic vital for Christian living.

The first volume looks at the promises of God through the lens of Edward Leigh, William Spurstowe, and Andrew Gray, each of whom wrote extensively, powerfully, and beautifully on this glorious subject. This book really has five authors—these three great divines plus Joel R. Beeke and James A. La Belle. Here is a brief biographical introduction to each Puritan contributor:

Edward Leigh (1603–1671)

Edward Leigh was born in 1603 in Shawell, Leicestershire, to Henry and Anne Leigh. His stepmother, Ruth Scudamore, introduced Edward to fervent Puritanism, which was further enhanced by his tutor, William Pemble (c. 1591–1623), a well-known Puritan minister. Edward's father supported him through Walsall grammar school, where he received a liberal education. Later, Leigh took on a double apprenticeship: first in Magdalen Hall (Oxford), graduating in 1620, and second in Middle Temple, beginning in 1624. His education was interrupted by the Great Plague in London in 1625. This gave Leigh an opportunity to travel for half a year in France.

In 1629, Leigh married Elizabeth Talbot. Their young son, Richard Leigh later became a well-known metaphysical poet. One of Leigh's earliest works of edification, *A Treatise of the Divine Promises* (1633), which we have gleaned from extensively in this book, was published when his children were very young.

In Banbury, Oxfordshire, Leigh became a supporter of the Puritan minister, William Whateley, who influenced Leigh to publish his *Prototypes* (1640). Eventually Leigh became known for his work in biblical exegesis, which benefited many Christians.

In 1640, Leigh returned to Staffordshire where he was appointed justice of the peace for the county in 1641. Because he was sympathetic towards parliament in his support of the Militia Bill, he was removed from service in 1642 by the royal command. That did not stop his political career, for he was soon appointed by Parliament to the honorable position of "keeper of the rolls" (*custos rotulorum*) i.e. keeper of the records, a position at that time regarded as one of the highest civil offices. By 1643 Leigh was engaged in the civil war, joining the parliamentary forces and even leading a regiment. In 1644, he gave the House of Commons a pro-Denbigh petition. The earl of Denbigh led a peace party faction, which Leigh supported. This was later published with a speech he gave, titled *A Speech of Colonell E. Leigh.*

In 1645, Leigh won a parliamentary election by a single vote, which upset some of his political opponents. As a member of parliament, Leigh increasingly became involved in ecclesiastical matters. He was a member of the committee of plundered ministers, visitor for the regulation of Oxford University, and chairman of a committee that investigated unlicensed ministers. He was also elected to the Westminster Assembly of divines. Though he attended the assembly as a teller, some viewed him as a "dangerous Presbyterian."

In 1648, during the civil war, Leigh was forcibly removed by the New Model Army during Pride's Purge on parliament for not supporting the Grandees or the Independents. He was kept prisoner for at least five weeks at Strand. For the next ten years, Leigh stayed out of political life because he disapproved of the regicide of Charles I and of Cromwell's ecclesiastical policies. When the Rump Parliament regained control, Leigh went back into public service, supporting the Restoration. Yet he ended up not being able to support the new government under Charles II.

Leigh died in June of 1671, in Rushall Hall. His last will to his immediate family, servants, tenants, and neighbors, was that they make true Christianity "their great business." He was remembered by contemporaries as a man of fiery disposition and cunning.

Leigh's major work, *Critica sacra,* was a philological study of biblical Hebrew and Greek. It was originally published in two editions, one in 1639 and the second in 1642. His other notable writings include his massive *A Treatise of Divinity* (1646), *The Saints' Encouragement in Evil Times* (1648), *Annotations Upon All the New Testament* (1650), *A Learned Discourse of Ceremonies Retained and Used in the Christian Churches* (1653), *A Philological Commentary* (1658), and *England Described* (1659). In 1661, after joining the Rump Parliament, Leigh wrote a historical study titled *Choyce Observations of all the Kings of England from the Saxons to the Death of King Charles the First.* His final book, *Three Diatribes or Discourses,* was published months before his death in 1671.[1]

William Spurstowe (c. 1605–1666)

William Spurstowe, the son of a London merchant, was admitted to Emmanuel College, Cambridge, in 1623, where he earned a bachelor's degree in 1627. He then moved to St. Catharine's College, Cambridge, where he received a master's degree three years later.

In 1638, Spurstowe entered the ministry at Great Hampden, Buckinghamshire, the church of the celebrated Parliamentary leader John Hampden. That same year he was also elected as a fellow of St. Catharine's College. A year or two later, he married a godly young woman named Sarah.

When the English civil war began, Spurstowe sided with Parliament and served as a chaplain (1642–43) in John Hampden's regiment,

---

1. Material for this biographical sketch draws primarily on John Sulton, "Leigh, Edward," *Oxford Dictionary of National Biography* (Oxford: Oxford University Press, 2004), 33:233–34.

under the command of the Earl of Essex. Like Hampden, he hoped to overthrow the king's forces in order to push the sovereign to a position more favorable to the Puritan conscience. Like most other royalist Puritans, neither Spurstowe nor Hampden was against the king himself—they never condoned his execution. After Hampden's untimely death in 1643, however, a process of events transpired that would culminate in the king's trial.

Spurstowe was one of five divines who wrote tracts against Episcopal church government in 1641 under the acronym *Smectymnuus*, the last three letters of this word forming his initials (VVS). The other authors were Stephen Marshall, Edmund Calamy, Thomas Young, and Matthew Newcomen. Reprinted at least four times by 1680, *Smectymnuus* contributed a note of conciliation into the ongoing debate between Episcopacy and Presbyterianism. Denying the apostolic origin of liturgies and the divine right of Episcopacy, its authors were willing to bear with the existence of bishops, if the office was reduced to its primitive simplicity. Furthermore, they were willing to allow liturgies on the condition that certain divines reform them according to God's Word. These conditions, however, were unacceptable to high churchmen.

Along with the other authors of *Symectymnuus*, Spurstowe was summoned to the Westminster Assembly of Divines. Shortly before the assembly convened on May 3, 1643, he succeeded Calybute Downing as preacher of St. John's, Hackney, Middlesex. The following year, he subscribed to the Solemn League and Covenant. Spurstowe served the assembly faithfully for several years, during which he preached before Parliament on at least four occasions.

Called a "grand Presbyterian" by his contemporaries, Spurstowe sat on the committee to consider the reasons given by the Independents for their views of church government. He was appointed a commissioner to Newport to confer with King Charles I in the Isle of Wight in 1648. Near the end of that year, he was one of the signers of a document drafted by Cornelius Burges (*A Vindication of the Ministers of the Gospel in, and about London*) vindicating the ministers of the gospel in London who opposed the anticipated trial of Charles I. Their pleas, however, were not heard; the king was executed for high treason in London on January 30, 1649.

Spurstowe was awarded a doctorate in divinity in 1649. The following year, he was deprived of his position as master of St. Catharine's for refusing allegiance to the existing government without a king or House of Lords. The renowned John Lightfoot succeeded him. After the Restoration, Lightfoot offered to resign in Spurstowe's favor, but Spurstowe declined.

In 1654, the Spurstowes lost their only son, William, at age nine to cholera. Simeon Ashe, a close friend, preached the funeral message, which was titled, "Christ: The Riches of the Gospel and the Hope of Christians." In the sermon, he describes how the young William was often much affected with heaven's glory and frequently spoke of the blessedness of being with Christ forever.

In the late 1650s, Spurstowe and a number of Presbyterian ministers supported Richard Cromwell. Spurstowe was appointed commissioner for the approbation of ministers in 1660, but that was soon disbanded with the Convention Parliament.

Spurstowe next assisted in the negotiations with Charles II in Holland in May 1660. Afterward, he was appointed chaplain-in-ordinary to Charles II, together with about ten other Presbyterian ministers. Of these, the king selected Spurstowe as one of four ministers to preach before him.

Ezekiel Hopkins became Spurstowe's assistant at Hackney in 1660. Spurstowe served as a commissioner to the Savoy Conference of April–July 1661. When the Act of Uniformity took effect on August 24, 1662, he resigned his living at Hackney, which then went to Thomas Jeamson. Spurstowe retired to his home in Hackney, living off his own means.

Having survived the plague of 1665, Spurstowe died suddenly the following year. His widow married Anthony Tuckney, a colleague from the Westminster Assembly.

Richard Baxter described Spurstowe as "an ancient, calm, reverend minister." Edmund Calamy praised him as "a man of great humility and meekness; and great charity both in giving and forgiving." According to James Reid, Spurstowe was a man with a peaceable disposition.

Spurstowe wrote three books: *The Wells of Salvation Opened: Or, A Treatise Discovering the nature, preciousness, usefulness of Gospel-Promises, and Rules for the right application of them* (1655); *The Spiritual Chymist; or, Six Decades of Divine Mediations* (1666), and *The Wiles of Satan* (1666). Only *The Wells of Salvation,* upon which much of this book is based, was reprinted in the seventeenth century (1659), and it may well be the best book ever written on God's promises. The book contains the content of several sermons, which Spurstowe introduces in a preface by saying: "The promises are a large field in which the wise merchant may find more pearls hidden, than are yet espied: a rich mine in which the diligent laborer may dig forth more fine gold, than any yet have taken from them."[2]

Andrew Gray (1633–1656)

Andrew Gray was born in Lawnmarket, Edinburgh, to Sir William of Pittendrum, a merchant and staunch royalist, and Egidia Smyth. He was the fourth son and eleventh child in a family of twenty-one. As a child, he was convicted of the sin of ingratitude by unexpectedly witnessing a beggar pour out his heart to God in a field near Leith. Before long, Gray was brought to rest in the finished work of Christ for his distraught soul.

Gray felt called to the ministry already as a boy. That gave impetus to his studies at Edinburgh and St. Andrews universities. He earned a Master of Arts degree in 1651 and, at age nineteen, was declared a candidate for the ministry. He was ordained in the Outer High Kirk in Glasgow by the Protestors on November 3, 1653, despite the objections of Robert Baillie and other Resolutioners.

Gray was regarded as a burning light by thousands who heard him preach. William Blaikie, author of *The Preachers of Scotland,* wrote, "His knowledge of Christian experience was wonderfully extensive and minute; he knew well the joys and troubles, the helps and hindrances, the temptations and elusions of the Christian life. He had a remarkable

2. Spurstowe, [viii–ix]. The Gray and Spurstowe sections of this introduction are adapted from Joel R. Beeke and Randall J. Pederson, *Meet the Puritans, with a Guide to Modern Reprints* (Grand Rapids: Reformation Heritage Books, 2006), 549–52, 704–708.

power of probing the conscience; as James Durham remarks, 'he could make men's hair stand on end.'"

Both in preaching and in his personal life, Gray exhibited the need for holiness. He was a genuinely pious man. George Hutcheson spoke of him as "a spark from heaven."

But that spark did not stay lit for long. Gray often preached of and longed for glory. When he was twenty-two, he expressed the desire that he would meet his Master in celestial bliss before his next birthday. Six months later, after a few days of fever, God granted that wish. Gray left behind a God-fearing wife, Rachel Baille (who later married George Hutcheson), and two children, Robert (who would soon die as a child) and Rachel. Gray's body was interred in Glasgow Cathedral.

"We may safely say that never in the history of our country did a man of his years make so deep a mark," said Blaikie. God used Gray mightily in his twenty-seven months of ministry.

Gray's writings have been collected and reprinted in two volumes. First, *The Works of Andrew Gray* (Ligonier, Penn.: Soli Deo Gloria, 1992), which contains several short books, originally preached as sermons, including *The Mystery of Faith Opened; Great and Precious Promises,* from which we have drawn in this book; *Directions and Instigations to the Duty of Prayer;* and *The Spiritual Warfare.* Second, *Loving Christ and Fleeing Temptation,*[3] which contains fifty sermons that demonstrate why Gray was so popular as a preacher. They make doctrine intelligible and practical; they powerfully speak to the mind and the conscience, comforting the regenerate, arresting the backslider, inviting the unsaved, and unmasking the hypocrite. Above all, they seek to win souls to Christ. As William Tweedie wrote, "Christ was the beginning, the middle, and the end of all his sermons."

Contemporary Style

We have footnoted direct quotations from these three authors. Most of the other material in the book summarizes their thoughts in a contem-

---

3. Edited by Joel R. Beeke and Kelly Van Wyck (Grand Rapids: Reformation Heritage Books, 2007).

porary form. Due to the target audience of these books — the common layperson — we have minimized footnote use in such cases. In a few instances, we have used other authors to fill in a few gaps, such as John Downame, Walter Marshall, Thomas Manton, and the Puritan-minded Octavius Winslow, but these are footnoted in full. Modern spelling and punctuation are used throughout. Study questions are added to facilitate group study.

Acknowledgments

Our heartfelt gratitude is extended first and foremost to our great God and Savior, for His wonderful, glorious, and beautiful promises showered upon believers in Christ Jesus. We would also like to thank our dear wives, Mary Beeke and Chantry La Belle, for their amazing loyalty to us, and to our patient and loving children (Calvin, Esther, and Lydia Beeke; River, Schylie, Forrest, Terra, Sandy, Rocky, and Chantry La Belle). Many thanks to Jerry Bridges for his helpful foreword to this volume and to David Kranendonk for supplying a select reading list of material on the promises of God that is still in print at this time. Thanks, too, to Phyllis TenElshof, Greg Bailey, and Rebecca VanDoodewaard for their helpful editing assistance and to Gary and Linda den Hollander, our excellent proofreading/typesetting team, as well as Amy Zevenbergen for the cover design.

If this book will serve to enable God's dear children to trust in God's promises more fully, drink from them more deeply, and live them out more consistently, our labor will be well rewarded.

—Joel R. Beeke and James A. La Belle

Abbreviations

Gray   Andrew Gray, "Great and Precious Promises," in *The Works of Andrew Gray* (repr., Ligonier, Pennsylvania: Soli Deo Gloria, 1992), 115–168.

Leigh   Edward Leigh, *A Treatise of the Divine Promises. In five Books. In the first, A general description of their nature, kinds, excellency, right use, properties, and the persons to whom they belong. In the four last, A declaration of the Covenant itself, the Bundle and Body of all the Promises, and the Special Promises likewise, which concern a man's self, or others, both Temporal, Spiritual, and Eternal* (London: A. Miller for Henry Mortlocke, 1657).

Spurstowe   William Spurstowe, *The Wells of Salvation Opened: Or, A Treatise Discovering the nature, preciousness, usefulness of Gospel-Promises, and Rules for the right application of them* (London: T. R. & E. M. for Ralph Smith, 1655).

Understanding the Promises of God

We love the Puritans and enjoy reading their writings. They have had an unmistakable influence on our lives and ministries. One reason they are so impressive is because God blessed them with profound insights into the truths of Scripture, which, in turn, produced appropriate and thorough applications. The Puritans sought to unfold the essence of truth for our understanding even as they drew attention to the wide-ranging influence of this truth for our practical application.

This is precisely the strength and enduring blessing of their treatment of God's promises. The Puritans do not speak about the applications or uses of God's promises until *after* they have instructed the mind and educated the understanding with regard to those promises. "Before we can *apply* the promises," they reason, "we must first *understand* their nature and various kinds, and appreciate their excellence and worth; we must know the foundation on which they are built and the spring from which they gush forth; we must be certain as to whom they belong and the various properties or characteristics inherent in them that urge both our faith in them and our use of them. Only with these track lights in place can we traverse such a broad terrain, avoiding both neglect and presumption, and encouraging both faith and use."

So our love for the promises of God begins with the Puritan understanding of their nature, their kinds, and their excellence and worth, for we are certain that the best structures begin with the best foundations. The tree left standing when the storm is passed is the one with the deepest roots.

The Nature of the Divine Promises

Edward Leigh began his treatise on the divine promises by saying the Word teaches us in three ways: through *precepts* or *commandments*, which teach obedience; *threats*, which restrain disobedience; and *promises*, which confirm our obedience.[1] The promises of God must be distinguished from His commandments and threats because the promises do not tell us our duty or what God will do if we fail in our duty. Rather, they confirm what God, motivated by His sovereign mercy and good pleasure, will do for us. Thus, a promise reveals a truth that will benefit us in particular. It declares God's will concerning the good with which He will bless us or the evil He will remove from us. The promises of God are a storehouse of blessings and a chest of goodwill bequeathed to us by our heavenly Father.

Leigh says the promises are "the grounds of our hope, the objects of our faith, and the rule of prayer."[2] We hope for what God has promised us because we are unable to look for anything besides what He has already declared He will bestow. If we hope for the things the Lord has promised us, our hope is solid. Without God's promises, we are either hopeless or overly hopeful.

The promises of God are likewise the objects of our faith in that we may believe whatever is promised because of the One who promised it. We may believe the promises of God because they are the promises of *God*, not the promises of man. Balaam urges this belief in God's promises in Numbers 23:19, saying: "God is not a man, that he should lie; neither the son of man, that he should repent: hath he said, and shall he not do it? Or hath he spoken, and shall he not make it good?" The promises of God are sure words to be believed because God stands behind them. Whatever is believed without a promise is only presumed (Heb. 11:11).

Finally, the promises of God are the rule of prayer. Just as we hope for and believe what God has promised, so we must pray for what God has promised. David makes this evident in 2 Samuel 7:27, when he prays, "For thou, O LORD of hosts, God of Israel, hast revealed to thy

---

1. Leigh, 1.
2. Ibid., 4–5.

servant, saying, I will build thee an house: therefore hath thy servant found in his heart to pray this prayer unto thee" (cf. Luke 1:38). Having the promise of God in hand not only emboldened David's hope and strengthened his faith, but it also fed and informed his prayer. Truly, we do not have a prayer without the promises of God.

Andrew Gray, in the first of five sermons on God's promises, defines a promise as "a glorious discovery of the *good-will* of God towards sinners, and withal, a *purpose* and *intendment*, and, if we may say, an *engagement*, to bestow some spiritual or temporal good upon them, or to withhold some spiritual or temporal evil from them."[3] In other words, a divine promise declares God's goodwill, purpose, and intention toward sinners. It reveals what the Lord our God *will* do on our behalf; not what He *hopes* to do or will *attempt* to perform, but what He has already committed and bound Himself to *accomplish* for us. Gray goes even further in using the word *engagement* to stress that the Lord, by making a promise, so binds and engages Himself to it that it will assuredly come to pass. This agrees with Leigh's point that the promises of God are promises of *truth*, for the certainty of their fulfillment rests in the One who made them and bound Himself to them.

William Spurstowe indicates much the same regarding the nature of God's promises when he says that a promise is "a declaration of God's will, wherein he signifies what particular good things he will freely bestow, and the evils that he will remove."[4] In this sense, a promise is a kind of "middle thing," Spurstowe says, between God's purpose and performance, between His intention of good and His execution of it upon those whom He loves. This is so inasmuch as the good that God purposes and intends to do for us, He reveals to us ahead of time by way of a promise, to grant us present comfort and to draw forth hope and expectancy. Thus, a promise is both the ground of present comfort and the expectation of future blessings.

Like Leigh, Spurstowe understands the importance of distinguishing God's promises from His threats and commands. A promise is different from a threat in that in a promise, God declares good rather than evil,

---

3. Gray, 117, emphasis added.
4. Spurstowe, 10.

and it is different from a command in that it concerns good things freely
bestowed rather than a duty to be done.

Furthermore, Spurstowe suggests that the promises are "irreversible
obsignations [seals] and declarations of God, which he has freely made"
to believers.[5] God's promises are objects of our faith and hope, for faith
believes those things that God has promised are true, and hope expects
the performance of what faith believes. We believe what God has promised because He has committed and bound Himself to act for us. We
hope for what we believe because our faith is rooted in the sure Word
spoken by Him who cannot lie.

As if singing three-part harmony, each of these Puritan friends sees
God's promises as sovereign declarations of good to be bestowed or evil
to be removed, which God makes known to us *prior* to their performance, so that we might enjoy comfort and assurance as we await the
fulfillment of His Word. However, while the divine promises enjoy this
essential unity as to their nature, there is a great diversity in the kinds
of promises the Lord has made. We should know and understand that
diversity so that we might profit from the promises as the Lord intends.

The Various Kinds of Divine Promises

In a most exhaustive yet helpful outline, Leigh suggests that the divine
promises are legal or evangelical, general or particular, principal or less
principal, direct or by consequence, absolute or conditional, and pertain
either to this life or the life to come. Similarly, Gray distinguishes the
promises as absolute or conditional; temporal, spiritual, or eternal; and
extraordinary—given to a particular believer as a singular privilege—or
common—promises to which every believer in Christ has a right.

Legal promises are conditioned on perfect righteousness. An example of such a promise can be found in Jeremiah 7:23: "But this thing
commanded I them, saying, Obey my voice, and I will be your God,
and ye shall be my people: and walk ye in all the ways that I have commanded you, that it may be well unto you." Given our sinful nature and
inability to keep a single command of God, this class of promises would

5. Ibid., 29.

be ineffective for us had not Christ, as our Head, Representative, and Savior, rendered the righteousness on which they depend for fulfillment. Through faith in Christ, we uphold the law of God (Rom. 3:31; 8:1–4) and thereby become heirs of these promises (Gal. 3:14, 29).

Evangelical promises are conditional on believing and repenting (John 3:36; 2 Cor. 7:10). Leigh says these promises are given "to the worker, not for the merit of his work, but for Christ's merit, in which both his person and work are accepted."[6] These promises are fulfilled, not for the sake of the person who believes or repents, as if those were meritorious acts in the sight of God, but rather because of Christ, the One in whom we have meritorious acceptance before God.

These two kinds of promises—legal and evangelical—are the root of all others. They not only show the importance of faith but make plain that the faith of those who inherit the promises of God must be in Christ, who alone has satisfied the righteous requirements of God's law. These promises are not for Christ but for those He came to save and to make partakers of the divine nature (2 Peter 1:4). Any other faith is misplaced and is therefore useless.

General promises are indefinite declarations of good that God offers to all. There is no limit on who may believe and receive such promises because God designed them as the refuge of many and a primary means of drawing sinners to Christ (John 6:44–45). Those who by the grace of God see their sin and great need for Christ are wooed by these unrestricted promises to believe that *even they* may look to Christ and find salvation. John 3:16 states such a general promise: "For God so loved the world, that he gave his only begotten Son, that whosoever believeth in him should not perish, but have everlasting life." By contrast, *particular* promises are directed to special groups of people. In Exodus 20:12, God promises long life only to those *children* who honor their fathers and mothers. Likewise, in Numbers 25:12–13, the Lord promises a perpetual priesthood only to zealous *Phinehas and his descendants.*

Principal promises are spiritual and therefore are of the greatest concern. They include the promise of righteousness (Rom. 4:5) and the

---

6. Leigh, 11.

remission of sins (1 John 1:9). *Less principal* promises are temporal and include promises such as deliverance from affliction, safety in danger, health, and wealth. Isaiah brought such a promise to Hezekiah when the Lord said, "Behold, I will add unto thy days fifteen years" (Isa. 38:5).

Direct promises are made to individuals, such as Paul on his tempestuous voyage to Rome (Acts 27:22–25), when an angel said to him, "Fear not, Paul; thou must be brought before Caesar: and, lo, God hath given thee all them that sail with thee" (v. 24). Promises implied or deduced by *consequences* are evident in the examples or prayers of faithful saints, since what God promises to one He promises to all who are in an equal state. For example, in James 5:11, James encourages us to remain patient in suffering by promising God's blessing to those who remain steadfast. He grounds that promise in the Lord's dealings with Job. In the same way, we discover promises in the prayers of the saints by considering those things for which they prayed and afterward obtained. As Leigh says: "The faithful calling upon God and God's gracious hearing of them are as much as a promise that God in such and such things will hear us calling upon him. David made this a ground of his faith [in] Psalm 22:4–5."[7] In addition, some promises can be distinguished as pertaining either to *this life*, whether spiritual or temporal, or to *the life to come*, such as the promise of eternal life.

Finally, and most importantly, we must distinguish between absolute and conditional promises. An *absolute* promise declares what the Lord determines to accomplish without any reference to what we do. Such a promise was indicated in Isaiah's prophecy about the virgin birth of Christ (7:14). The Lord made this promise absolutely and sovereignly. Another example is the absolute promise of a flood that the Lord made to Noah in Genesis 6:13.

Conditional promises, by contrast, are "no further promised than God in wisdom sees to be best for his own glory and his children's good."[8] In this conditional way, subject to His glory and our good, the Lord promises all temporal blessings (which Lazarus lacked), freedom from all crosses and troubles (which Job suffered), freedom from

---

7. Ibid., 12.
8. Ibid., 13.

temptation (which even Christ faced), less principal graces and the common gifts of the Spirit (which are variously distributed, 1 Cor. 12:8), and sanctifying grace (which varies among saints). All of these blessings are promised, but they are conditional on what God knows to be best for His glory and our good in particular situations.

Thus, absolute promises make known a certain and sovereign purpose, while conditional promises reveal what God will do if the fulfillment of those promises glorifies Him and is best for His people. We might say that with absolute promises we are passive recipients of God's sovereign pleasure, while with conditional promises something is first required of us. If we fail to meet this requirement, we may lose much spiritual comfort.

In discussing the important distinction between absolute and conditional promises, Gray says that absolute promises, such as God's sending His Son into the world, have no condition annexed to the performance of them, while conditional promises, such as the promise that he who believes shall be saved, require some condition to be met by the Christian before the promise is fulfilled. Gray then reminds us, "Yet there is not a conditional promise that is in all the covenant of grace, but it may be reduced into an absolute promise, in regard that the *thing* promised ...is an absolute free gift, and the *condition* of the promise is another."[9] In other words, the root of divine promises is the sovereign goodness of God by which He purposes and engages Himself to do good to sinners, not because of any merit in them, but out of free grace, since even the condition required (faith, repentance, or the like) is itself of God (2 Tim. 2:25; Acts 13:48; John 6:44–45, 65). Gray's words remind us of what Augustine prayed: "Command what Thou wilt, and give what Thou wilt command."[10]

What is the benefit of distinguishing between all of these kinds of promises? Leigh says that as "tradesmen sort their commodities, by which they live; so should believers sort their promises, upon which they trust."[11] Some promises, such as Isaiah 40:31, offer encouragement;

---

9. Gray, 117, emphasis added.
10. http://www.christianitytoday.com/ct/2002/juneweb-only/6-24-53.0.html
11. Leigh, 16.

some, such as 1 Corinthians 10:13, give comfort; some bring rewards (Ps. 84:11); and some, privileges (John 1:12). Knowing what kind of promise we are dealing with not only guides us in appropriating it but also guards us against the evil of presumption.

The Excellence and Worth of the Divine Promises

Nothing is so excellent, so precious, and so sweet as a promise of God. The Scriptures call the promises the unsearchable riches of Christ, the bonds of love, and the inheritance of God's people. They are "a rich mine of spiritual and heavenly treasures; a garden of [the] most precious flowers [and] medicinal herbs; they are as the Pool of Bethesda for all diseases, for all sorts of persons, and at all times."[12]

Leigh says the promises are precious because God is the Author who gave them and Christ is the One who purchased them. They are precious in the free manner in which they are given and in the great and inestimable profit that flows from them. They are also precious because they promise eternal glory and virtue, and because through them we become partakers of the divine nature (2 Peter 1:4).

Gray identifies eight respects in which the promises are exceedingly precious. They are precious, first, because of the great price that was laid down for them, which was the blood of Christ. Second, they are precious because of the great things that are promised in them. Third, they are precious because of the great advantage afforded to a Christian who enjoys them. They are "the pencils that draw the ... lineaments of the image of Christ upon the soul."[13] Fourth, they are precious because of their close relationship with Jesus Christ, for what are the promises but streams and rivulets that flow from Him? As Gray asks, "Can this fountain that is sweet in itself, send forth any bitter waters?"[14]

Fifth, the promises are precious because they are the objects of faith, the precious mother of all graces. Sixth, the promises guide and lead us to Christ, for there is not a single promise that does not cry out to us

---

12. Ibid.
13. Gray, 157.
14. Ibid.

in a loud voice, "O, come to Christ!" and there is no access to Jesus but by a promise. Seventh, the saints of all ages have found great sweetness and unspeakable delight in the promises. Eighth, the saints have a high and matchless account of the promises and thereby commend them to us. How can we doubt the preciousness of God's promises when these arguments surround us like a cloud of witnesses?[15]

Spurstowe summarizes the excellence and preciousness of the promises in three main points. He says, first, the promises are precious because Christ is the root and principle from which the promises spring. Second, they are the objects of faith, through which they feed, nurture, and sustain every other grace. Third, the promises are precious because of what they contain to interest believers and give them a right to believe. Thus, we come full circle out of Christ and back to Christ: from Christ to the promises, from the promises to faith, and from faith to the things promised, the chief of which is Christ Himself, in whom are all other blessings!

Finally, as to the great and immeasurable worth of God's promises, Spurstowe suggests that while the principle of every believer's life is faith in Christ, the means of its preservation are the promises.[16] From our implantation into Christ at the first to our full enjoyment of Him at the last, God's promises are the chief aids to our life and our growth. Using 1 John 2:12–14 ("Little children, young men, and fathers") as three stages of the Christian life, Spurstowe shows how the promises are suited to all phases of life. He says:

> The promises are the *babe's* milk by which they are nourished, the full breasts from which they suck both grace and comfort; they are the *young men's* evidences, by which they are animated to combat with the wicked one, and assured of being crowned with victory over him; they are the *old men's* staff, upon the top of which like aged Jacob they may safely lean, and worship God; it being a staff for power like Moses' rod, and for flourishing like Aaron's [rod], budding, blossoming, and yielding precious fruit. So that it is of more than ordinary concernment unto every one of them that look upon themselves as

15. Ibid., 157–58.
16. Spurstowe, 2.

believers...not to be supine [i.e., negligent] and careless in the frequent use, and due application of the promises.[17]

We have now sketched with a Puritan pen the nature of God's promises, the various categories into which they are grouped, and why they are so precious to us. With these three points in mind, we already have a better understanding of the divine promises than we did before. Yet we have barely scratched the surface of what the Puritans taught. If such gems and treasures are so readily apparent on the surface of our study, what diamonds will be found in its source? What sweetness can we expect at the fountainhead if the waters that flow from it are so profitable? Let us then follow the stream to its source.

Study Questions

1. Why do you think the Puritans wrote so extensively on the promises of God? Why are believers today prone to make so much less of God's promises?

2. Why should God's promises be an important part of the life of His children? If you are a believer, why are you often reticent to plead on God's promises? How could you make more use of the promises than you presently do?

3. Edward Leigh says God's promises are "the grounds of our hope, the objects of our faith, and the rule of prayer." What does he mean by that? In what ways is each of these expressions true?

4. What encouragement should we glean from Andrew Gray's observation that God's promises imply God's goodwill, purpose, and intention toward sinners?

---

17. Ibid., 2–3.

5. What does William Spurstowe mean by saying that a promise of God is a "middle thing" between God's purpose and God's performance?

6. How do God's promises differ from His threats and His commands?

7. How would you define God's promises?

8. Why is it important to distinguish what kind of promise we are dealing with when reading the Scriptures?

9. Explain the difference between *conditional* promises and *absolute* promises. Explain how God's conditional promises are rooted in His absolute promises. How does your explanation prevent you from falling into an Arminian view of God's promises?

10. List ten precious promises contained in the Bible. (For help, look at some verses in Edward Leigh's appended "Table of Promises.") Provide ten reasons why these promises should be exceedingly precious to believers (2 Pet. 1:4).

The Foundation and
Fountainhead of God's Promises

I (James La Belle) was in construction for many years and built many houses, from low cost to very expensive. My goal in every case was to build a house of exceptional quality at a reasonably safe speed. That gave both the homeowner and me a place of which we could be grateful.

With each project, the first days were the most critical, though I built nothing in that time beyond a set of sawhorses and a blueprint table. However, during this time I also evaluated the *foundation* that had been laid and on which I had to build. I took special care to measure the length of every wall, the distance between walls, the height of every step-down, the placement of every bearing point, and the location of every beam pocket. I double- and triple-checked each corner to make sure it was square, then found the biggest perfect square off which I could confidently measure every other square. Finally, I used my laser-level to make sure the foundation was perfectly level.

Why go through all that fuss while sacrificing time that could be spent building? After all, if the foundation was out of square or out of level, was not that the concrete company's problem?

The answer is no. Whatever problems the foundation had, as I used to say, would "follow me to the roof." Any corner out of square would give me a problem in the walls that met at that corner, in the windows placed in those walls, and in the roof nailed to the walls at that corner. The siding installer would complain about that corner. So would the sheetrock installer, the trim carpenter, the cabinet installer, the appliance installer, and the flooring installer. Every subcontractor would complain because each would have to adjust the out-of-square corner to keep the homeowner from complaining!

—⟫•◆•⟪—

I (Joel Beeke) worked for my Dad as a teenager. My Dad, who was a contractor, often confirmed what James La Belle writes above, speaking to me about the importance of the foundation of a house. One time he asked, "Son, of the more than one hundred people I built homes for in the last thirty years, how many do you think asked about what kind of foundation I laid?"

"Thirty?" I said.

"Lower," he said.

"Ten?" I asked.

"Only one. People asked about all kinds of things before they signed off on me as a builder, down to the color of shutters, but only one ever asked what kind of foundation I built."

Then Dad continued: "There's a parallel here to spiritual foundations. In my thirty years of experience as a ruling elder, I've discovered that very few Christians today seriously ask whether they are building on the foundational Rock, Christ Jesus. Many are concerned about how they feel and what they experience, but few ask about what kind of foundation they are building on. As a future preacher, son, you need to talk to people about the foundation of their salvation, for if they get that wrong, they will get everything else wrong, too."

My Dad concluded: "And there's no group of writers in my bookcase that consistently lay a better foundation for souls traveling to eternity than the Puritans. Read those books, son; you'll never be sorry."

I did read them, or shall I say, I devoured them—night after night, often well beyond midnight. And I'm still reading them now, forty years later. My Dad was right: the foundation of a house is important, but the foundation of our eternal hope is far more important. The foundation on which we rest our confidence and build our trust is absolutely critical.

If we are Christians, praise be to God that neither our hope, nor our trust, nor our confidence are based on a foundation built by man, but rather are grounded securely on the promises of God. And praise God that those promises are built on the foundation of the covenant of grace by which God has bound Himself to be our God and, by the mediation of Jesus Christ, joined us to Himself as His people. So let us look at, first, the foundation, and second, the fountainhead and spring of God's promises.

The Foundation of the Divine Promises

Edward Leigh says the covenant of grace is the foundation of all Christian hope. He refers to this covenant as a "bundle of all the promises."[1] Whatever promise is made to believers in Scripture, it is nothing less than an explication and application of the foundational promise of the covenant, namely, "I...will be their God, and they shall be my people" (Jer. 31:33).

That promise was given from the time when God chose Abraham as head of the nation through which Christ was to come. The Lord stirred Abraham's hope by promising *Himself*. He said, "Fear not, Abram, I am thy shield; and thy exceeding great reward" (Gen. 15:1). Later, the Lord extended this promise to Abraham's offspring, Isaac and Jacob, saying, "I will establish my covenant between me and thee and thy seed after thee in their generations for an everlasting covenant, to be a God unto thee, and to thy seed after thee" (Gen. 17:7; cf. Gen. 20:3; 28:13–15; 35:11–12; Ps. 105:8–10).

Just how foundational this covenant relationship is becomes clear in Exodus 2, where it is given as the reason *why* God delivered the Israelites from Egypt. In verses 23–25, Moses writes: "And it came to pass in process of time, that the king of Egypt died: and the children of Israel sighed by reason of the bondage, and they cried, and their cry came up unto God by reason of the bondage. And God heard their groaning, and God remembered his covenant with Abraham, with Isaac, and with Jacob. And God looked upon the children of Israel, and God had

---

1. Leigh, 103.

respect unto them" (cf. Ps. 105:8, 37–42). For more than four hundred years, God's promises to the patriarchs had appeared to be null and void. But God had not forgotten His Word and His covenant. The Israelites' sojourn in Egypt all those years was part of God's sovereign plan that He had revealed to Abraham in Genesis 15:13–14. What God had long ago purposed, He would now perform.

But did God merely deliver His people as He promised? No. He brought to fruition the *relationship* He had long ago established with them. His first act on their behalf (besides protecting and multiplying them in Egypt) was delivering them from slavery and from the "gods" who lorded over them. He then brought them into the land of Canaan, where He would be their God and where they would enjoy all the benefits of being His people (cf. Ps. 105:43–45).

God's covenant promise to Abraham in Genesis 15 secured a relationship with the people of Israel, according to which He now distinguished them from all other nations and peoples (Ex. 33:15–16) as His people, His treasured possession. The effect of that covenant promise for Israel, which He began to fulfill in their deliverance, is summarized in Romans 9:4–5, where Paul says, "Who are Israelites; to whom pertaineth the adoption, and the glory, and the covenants, and the giving of the law, and the service of God, and the promises; whose are the fathers, and of whom as concerning the flesh Christ came, who is over all, God blessed for ever."

In other words, not only the deliverance from Egypt but all the divine revelation and blessings that became a part of the Israelite identity from that day forward were built on that foundational promise of a covenant relationship, whereby God bound Himself to Abraham's offspring to be their God, their shield, and their very great reward. God heard the cries of the Israelites in Egypt because they were *His* people, and God answered their cries because He had promised to be *their* God. His answer was not *mere* deliverance but deliverance *from* bondage *unto* all heavenly and divine blessedness; it was an adoption, a reception into a relationship that proved to be immeasurably fruitful.

This relationship grounded for them *then* and still grounds for us *today* all of God's promises, because the core of a divine promise is not so much the thing promised but God Himself. The promises bring us into an unshakable, inviolable, and fruitful relationship with God. As Leigh says, "When a man has God, he has all, [for] he is blessedness itself."[2] William Spurstowe puts it this way: "The promises are instrumental in the coming of Christ and the soul together; they are the *warrant* by which faith is emboldened to come to him and to take hold of him; but the union which faith makes is not between a believer and the promise, but between a believer and Christ...for the object of faith is not...an evangelical maxim or proposition; but...the person of Christ,"[3] which is to say, God Himself.

All of God's promises depend on the truth that God is our God, for only this relationship can secure those things that the promises hold out to us. So Leigh says: "He that is in special covenant with God, all that is in God is for him: his truth for his security; his love for his comfort; his power for his protection; his wisdom for his direction. All that is in Christ is his, his love, his graces, his merits. He is his Savior [and] Redeemer; the Holy Ghost is his Comforter [and] dwells in him, to teach him and guide him into all truth, and to seal up the promises to his heart."[4] Thus, particular promises are built on the foundation of the covenant of grace and take their security from its strength and stability.

Likewise, every scriptural promise is sealed with the assurance that God is our God, for without God being our God, everything is a misery. Even the rich and wonderful promises of Leviticus 26 find their conclusion in the promise of verse 12, "And I will walk among you, and will be your God, and ye shall be my people." What good would be a bountiful harvest, peace in the land, and posterity without the presence of God? Temporal things pass away with their using and can in no way compare with the honor and happiness of having God as our God. As Scripture says: "Happy art thou, O Israel: who is like unto thee, O people saved by the LORD, the shield of thy help, and who is the sword of thy excellency!" "Blessed is the nation whose God is the LORD; and the people whom he hath chosen for his own inheritance!" "Blessed is the man

---

2. Leigh, 110.
3. Spurstowe, 45.
4. Leigh, 105–106.

whom thou choosest, and causest to approach unto thee, that he may dwell in thy courts: we shall be satisfied with the goodness of thy house, even of thy holy temple" (Deut. 33:29; Pss. 33:12; 65:4).

Thus, if we steadfastly believe and rest on the foundational promise that *God is our God*, we will find more comfort than we could find in all the world. David expresses this beautifully in Psalm 56:8–11: "Thou tellest my wanderings: put thou my tears into thy bottle: are they not in thy book? When I cry unto thee, then shall mine enemies turn back: this I know; for God is for me. In God will I praise his word: in the LORD will I praise his word. In God have I put my trust: I will not be afraid what man can do unto me." Caught in the gap between God's promise (1 Sam. 16:11–13) and its fulfillment, David finds a world of comfort in the foundational promise of God that *God is for him*.

There is no greater proof of the blessedness and felicity of this relationship than the words by which God refers to those who will be in covenant with Him and the benefits this relationship secures. We are His own possession (Ps. 135:4), His portion and allotted heritage (Deut. 32:9), His treasured ones (Ps. 83:3), the apple of His eye (Zech. 2:8), His beloved ones (Pss. 108:6; 127:2), those engraved on the palms of His hands (Isa. 49:16), and those with whom He dwells (John 14:23). Of His chosen ones, God promises to stand at our right hand and uphold us by it (Pss. 109:31; 73:23), hide us in His shelter in the day of trouble (Ps. 27:5), guard our feet and keep our bones (1 Sam. 2:9; Ps. 34:20), number the hairs of our heads and put our tears in His bottle (Matt. 10:30; Ps. 56:8), and be the shield of our help and the sword of our triumph (Deut. 33:29). He is our hope, our refuge, and our stronghold (Ps. 71:5; Joel 3:16), and our rock and fortress (Ps. 62:2). He will instruct us in the way we should go and make us perfect in good works (Ps. 25:12; Heb. 13:21). He will give us the desires of our hearts (Ps. 37:4) and will keep His eye ever upon us for good (Ps. 33:18).

Our hope and belief in the promises of God, then, are built on the inviolable and unshakable relationship that God has established with us through Christ in the covenant of grace. We must view the divine promises on this ground and plead what we will on the basis that God has committed Himself to us as our Father (Matt. 6:9; Gal. 4:5–6) and obligated Himself to care for us (Ps. 84:11). We must remind Him of His covenant and press Him with His promises (Phil. 4:6; Ps. 119:156).

Not for our sake but for His own name's sake we may expect to receive protection in dangers and distresses (Ps. 80:14–16), to have our needs supplied (Ps. 23), to boldly challenge sin, death, hell, and the devil, knowing that we will triumph over them all (1 Cor. 15:55–57), and to say with David, "The LORD is my light and my salvation; whom shall I fear?" (Ps. 27:1). These are our rights and privileges as the children of God, the recipients of His grace, through which He has sovereignly brought us into covenant with Himself (Gal. 3:29; Zech. 13:9).

When Moses spoke to the Israelites about their election as God's treasured possession, he appealed to God's covenant, saying, "But because the LORD...would keep the oath which he had sworn unto your fathers, hath the LORD...redeemed you.... Know therefore that the LORD thy God, he is God, the faithful God, which keepeth covenant" (Deut. 7:8–9). When Nehemiah heard about the destruction of Jerusalem, he was driven to pray. He began by appealing to God's covenant with Israel: "O LORD God of heaven, the great and terrible God, that keepeth covenant...let thine ear now be attentive, and thine eyes open, that thou mayest hear the prayer of thy servant" (Neh. 1:5–6). Likewise, when Daniel sought the Lord on behalf of His exiled people, he, too, grounded his request in an appeal to God's covenant promise: "O Lord, the great and dreadful God, keeping the covenant.... Let thine anger and thy fury be turned away.... Defer not, for thine own sake, O my God: for thy city and thy people are called by thy name" (Dan. 9:4, 16, 19).

How can we doubt the certainty of a single promise when all of God's promises are built on His sure word, His condescension, and His sovereign essence? This foundation will bear all our hope, all our trust, and all our confidence. On this foundation we can build our entire Christian lives. It is the foundation on which we *must* build if we would be saved (Ps. 130:7).

The Fountainhead and Spring of the Divine Promises

If the foundation of the promises of God is His covenant promise to be *our God*, then the fountainhead from which they flow to us is Christ. Our covenant relationship with God is effected in us and for us through Christ's mediation and saving work. Without the saving work of Christ, we remain enemies of God (Rom. 5:10) and stand outside the reach of God's promises (John 3:36).

Spurstowe and Andrew Gray go into great detail as to how Christ is the fountain from which divine promises flow to us. As we examine their teachings, we must keep two points in mind: one, that Christ is the Head of the church who receives the promises, and, two, that Christ is the Savior of sinners who apportions the promises to those He saves.

On the first point, Spurstowe writes, "[Christ] is the *Alpha* and *Omega* of all the promises, the only Original from whence they spring, and the centre in which they meet. To him they were all first made and ratified on our behalf; in him they are all fulfilled and accomplished unto us. As the rivers have their *efflux* from the sea and their *reflux* into the sea; so have the promises their *emanation* from Christ, their *revolution* into Christ; they *flow* freely from him, they *lead* sweetly to him."[5] Later he says that Christ is the root and principle from whom the promises spring, explaining: "They are as so many beams of Christ the Sun of righteousness and do impart a light which discovers his excellency, evidences our propriety, and effects in us a blessed purity. They are the desirable fruit of the tree of life...in the midst of the City of God ...they are the crystal streams of that river of life which proceeded out of the Throne of God and the Lamb (Rev. 22:1)."[6]

Overwhelmed with the blessedness of this truth, Spurstowe goes on to the second point, that Christ alone apportions the promises of God to believers. He reflects:

> Oh! how happy is every believer, whose light is the love of Christ shining in the rays of the promises; whose food is the tree of life that continually yields fruit both new and various; whose cordials are the waters of life, not sparingly given to a bare sustentation, but freely

---

5. Spurstowe, 4.
6. Ibid., 15–16.

flowing to a delightful satiety! Well might David in a rapture say to God: "What is man, that thou art mindful of him? and the son of man, that thou visitest him? For thou hast made him a little lower than the angels" (Ps. 8:4–5). Well also might Paul as one standing upon the shore and fathoming the sea of God's mercy cry out, "O the depth of the riches both of the wisdom and knowledge of God!" (Rom. 11:33). And most joyfully may every heir of the promise say, "The lines are fallen unto me in pleasant places; yea, I have a goodly heritage" (Ps.16:6), to whom such precious promises are given, as exceed both in glory and certainty all earthly performances whatever, being in Christ from whom they all come, yea, and amen (2 Cor. 1:20).[7]

Gray speaks on this matter in the second of his five sermons on 2 Peter 1:4, giving six respects in which Christ is the fountainhead of the promises of God. First, He is the fountainhead because He purchased the promises by His own blood. "There is not a promise in all the everlasting covenant but it is the price of the blood of the Son of God," Gray writes.[8] This is made clear in Ephesians 2:12, which says the Gentiles were strangers to the covenants of promise, but this alienation was remedied "by the blood of Christ" (v. 13). Ephesians 3:6 says we partake of the promises "in Christ Jesus through the gospel," or through the reconciliation secured by His death on the cross (Eph. 2:16). Finally, 1 Peter 1:19 tells us we were ransomed "with the precious blood of Christ," which means that the promise of our redemption (Ezek. 6:6; Luke 2:38; Rom. 3:24) is secured by the price of Christ's blood.

Second, Christ is the fountainhead because He is the One to whom the promises of the covenant were first made, and through Him they are given to us. Gray says, "The promises are not given to Christ considered only as the Son of God…but yet they are first made to Him as the Mediator and head of the church, and as that blessed daysman[9]… and we all receive of His fullness."[10]

---

7. Ibid., 16–17.
8. Gray, 126.
9. A mediator, cf. Job 9:33.
10. Gray, 126.

This is important for us to understand. The Puritan Thomas Goodwin says only two men stand before God, the first and second Adam, and we all hang from their girdles (or belts). Christ is the Son of Man and Head of the church, to whom God the Father has promised all blessings for us. We have a right to the promises of God only as we are found in Christ. What God promised to man, He promised to Christ the Son of Man, and through Him, by grace, we have those promises in Him. Of Christ alone God can and did say, "Thou art my beloved Son, in whom I am well pleased" (Mark 1:11). We hang upon the promise of Christ that He said to the Father, "I have declared unto them thy name, and will declare it: that the love wherewith thou hast loved me may be in them, and I in them" (John 17:26). Moreover, Paul states plainly in Galatians 3:16 that the promises of the covenant of grace made to Abraham and his offspring were made to Christ, so that any benefits that the Israelites enjoyed from the promises were due to their belonging to Christ, to whom the promises rightfully and singularly belong.

Third, Christ is the fountainhead of the promises of God because in Him we have a right to all the promises (1 Cor. 3:22–23). Gray says, "If once a soul close[s] with Christ in the covenant of promise, there is not one promise in Scripture but he may write this superscription above it, *this is mine*, this is mine."[11] What an inexhaustible store is laid up for the believer in Christ!

Fourth, Christ is the fountainhead because He makes us rest on the promises and believe in them. He gives rest to His people in the promises (Matt. 11:28), causes us to believe in His Word (Mark 9:24), and applies the good things of God offered in the promises (Rev. 3:18). David asks God to remember His word, in which God has made him hope (Ps. 119:49). Gray says it is as if David says, "*I had never believed a promise, except thou hadst caused me.*"[12]

Fifth, Christ is the fountainhead because He qualifies us for the accomplishment of the promises and infuses habitual grace in us by which we may exercise faith upon them. If Christ did not help us, we would never believe a single promise offered in Scripture, and not a single

---

11. Ibid., 126.
12. Ibid., 127.

promise would be accomplished for us. Christ qualifies us to receive the promises by calling us unto Himself (John 5:25), then gives us grace to believe and hope in all that God has promised (Acts 16:14; Phil. 1:29).

Finally, Christ is the fountainhead of the promises because all the promises of the covenant are accomplished through Him. As the apostle says in 2 Corinthians 1:20, "For all the promises of God in him are yea, and in him Amen." No wonder Christ calls us to Himself (Matt. 11:28), no wonder the Father draws us unto Christ (John 6:44–45), and no wonder the Holy Spirit unites us with Christ (Rom. 8:11), for as Leigh says (referring to Gen. 3:15), "The first promise was made concerning Christ, because God intended to make good every promise in Christ."[13] Similarly, Spurstowe says that a promise cannot be enjoyed without closing with Christ: "As we cannot come to Christ without the aid of a promise, so we may not rest in a promise without closing with Christ."[14]

Thus, the promises of God are grounded on the foundational covenant promise that God is *our* God, which entitles us to all that God is, since in His promises He gives us Himself. These promises have Christ for their fountainhead since they are rightly His as the Head of the church. All promises therefore not only flow from Him, but happily for us, also lead to Him.

The questions we might ask at this point are: Who may rightly rest in the promises of God? To whom do they rightly and properly belong? Can any apply for them? Can any make his suit to God with promise in hand? Are they always applicable, for all times, under all circumstances, and for all people? These are critical questions for us to consider, for with all the excellence and worth of the promises, God has not given them so that we might only prize their beauty. Rather, He has given them so we might find consolation and comfort in them and be led by them to Christ. Let us then turn to the question of to whom the promises of God belong, even as we look to God that they might be ours.

---

13. Leigh, 237.
14. Spurstowe, 46.

Study Questions

1. Foundations of homes are important but often neglected by prospective home buyers. Why are spiritual foundations even more important? Why do these also tend to be neglected?

2. According to the Puritans, what is the most important foundation of God's promises?

3. If an unbeliever walked into church and heard your minister preach about the covenant of grace and covenant theology, then asked you after the church service, "What do the *covenant of grace* and *covenant theology* mean," how would you answer?

4. How does the truth that "God is our God in Christ" serve as the foundation of God's promises and the foundation of the covenant of grace?

5. Our covenant-keeping God calls His people many wonderful names in Scripture. List twenty such names with scriptural support, including at least five that are not listed in chapter 2. How do these names multiply the believer's hope and sense of security?

6. Old Testament saints often appealed to God's covenant when pleading for personal or national mercy. How should we do that today? Why is pleading on God's character and covenant more effective than pleading upon ourselves or any of our accomplishments?

7. Name six ways in which Christ is God's fountain from which His promises flow to us. Explain why that comforts you.

8. What did Thomas Goodwin mean when he said that only two men stand before God, the first and second Adam, and we all hang from their belts?

9. Explain how all the promises of the covenant are accomplished through Jesus Christ.

10. Explain why the covenant of grace lies at the heart of all of Scripture. How does that covenant affect your own heart?

The People to Whom God's Promises Belong

When a wealthy landowner dies, who has the right to his estate? When the owner of a multimillion-dollar franchise dies, who inherits what is left behind?

Relationship decides the question, whenever possible. The one most closely related to the deceased has the greatest right to the inheritance. The privilege of ownership falls to the one in direct relation to the benefactor. If a benefactor has no natural heirs, he might name others to whom his goods will be bequeathed. This naming has the force of law behind it, making certain that his possessions will be given with full rights and privileges to those he names as beneficiaries.

In this chapter we will consider who has a right to God's promises and then grapple with the problem of delay in the fulfillment of those promises. Finally, we will conclude with a call to faith for those yet outside of Christ.

A Right to the Promises of God

To whom do the promises of Christ belong and to whom does our Lord bequeath them? The answer to this question is crucial. We have already established the excellence and worth of God's promises and the precious healing graces that flow from them. So the answer to this question of right and privilege which is now before us must be dealt with in some detail.

Let us explain. We have already established that the promises of God rightly belong to Christ as the only begotten Son of God, for the Father has said, "This is my beloved Son, in whom I am well pleased" (Matt. 3:17), and it is to Him that the Father has promised all things, saying, "Thou art my Son…. Ask of me, and I shall give thee the heathen for thine inheritance, and the uttermost parts of the earth for thy possession" (Ps. 2:7–8). The Father has appointed Christ, His Son, as "heir of all things" (Heb. 1:2), and Scripture speaks of Christ as He "for whom are all things" (Heb. 2:10). These promises belong to Christ not merely as the Son of God, but also as the appointed Mediator and Head of the church.

As much as the promises of God properly and rightly belong to Christ, they also properly and rightly belong to the church, which is His body (Eph. 1:22–23; 1 Cor. 12:12–13, 27). As Edward Leigh writes, the covenant of grace is first made with Christ as Head of the church, but it is next made with all Christian men and women who are united with Christ by grace through faith. Leigh says, "The promises made to Christ are, *Thou shalt be a priest forever, and I will give thee the Kingdom of David;* thou shalt be a *Prince of Peace, and the government shall be upon thy shoulders;* thou shalt be a *Prophet to my people,* [and] *shalt open the prison to the captive…*[whereas] the promises made to [His body] are passive, *You shall be taught, you shall be made prophets, you shall have your sins forgiven, you shall be subject to his government,* [and] *you shall be made kings."*[1]

Thus, all the good of the promises comes to us as believers *because we belong to Christ* and upon no other ground. The apostle Paul says, "All things are yours…and ye are Christ's; and Christ is God's" (1 Cor. 3:21–23). Elsewhere, he writes: "Even so we, when we were children, were in bondage under the elements of the world: but when the fulness of the time was come, God sent forth his Son, made of a woman, made under the law, to redeem them that were under the law, that we might receive the adoption of sons. And because ye are sons, God hath sent forth the Spirit of his Son into your hearts, crying, Abba, Father.

---

1. Leigh, 82–83.

Wherefore thou art no more a servant, but a son; and if a son, then an heir of God through Christ" (Gal. 4:3–7).

Lest we think this benefit belongs to us as we are in ourselves, Paul reminds us in Romans 8 that the privilege belongs to us only as we belong to Christ. He says: "There is therefore now no condemnation to them which are in Christ Jesus…. But ye have received the Spirit of adoption…. The Spirit itself beareth witness with our spirit, that we are the children of God: and if children, then heirs; heirs of God, and joint-heirs with Christ; if so be that we suffer with him, that we may also be glorified together" (vv. 1, 15–17).

Therefore, God's promises belong to us, not because we are by nature related to God, but because we have been named and brought into relation with Him by the grace of adoption. Westminster Shorter Catechism puts it this way: "Adoption is an act of God's free grace, whereby we are received into the number, and have a right to all the privileges, of the sons of God" (Q. 34). That heavenly store, to which we had no access because of our sins, has become ours because God has adopted us in Jesus Christ as His children. Paul says, "By whom also we have access by faith into this grace wherein we stand" (Rom. 5:2). Therefore, we who are joined to Christ by saving faith stand in relation to the promises of God as children of God. Absolutely nothing stands in the way of our full access to and enjoyment of the promises of God!

That said, we should also note that those outside of Christ are excluded from His promises. They have no right to the rich heritage of the saints because they do not belong to Him to whom the promises belong (cf. Acts 8:21–22). As Leigh concludes: "The Devil sweeps [away] all that are out of the Covenant; the children's bread shall not be given to dogs; God will not cast away precious things upon swine and those that are *strangers from the covenants of promise* (Eph. 2:12). God promises to satisfy, but such as hunger for righteousness sake; to comfort, not the careless, but such as mourn; forgiveness of sins, but to the penitent; eternal life, but to such as believe. *Except the condition be wrought in us, the promise shall never be accomplished upon us.*"[2]

---

2. Ibid.

On the other hand, whatever the promises are, they cannot fail to be accomplished upon us who belong to Christ, because they have been given to Him as our Mediator, not as conditional promises, but as absolute promises and sure words (Heb. 6:13, cf. Gal. 3:16). Leigh explains: "This is a comfort to the people of God; they can never lose the evangelical blessings of grace and glory, because Christ is made the *Lord Treasurer* and *Lord Keeper* of them. We are not trusted with them ourselves, for then we should lose them; but he receives them for us, and communicates them to us."[3]

The guarantee of the fulfillment of these promises to us is Christ's exaltation in our human flesh as the Son of Man, not merely for Himself, but that He might bring "many sons to glory" (Heb. 2:10). Those sons are "begotten again unto a lively hope...to an inheritance incorruptible, and undefiled, and that fadeth not away, reserved in heaven for you, who are kept by the power of God through faith unto salvation ready to be revealed in the last time," and, therefore, are sure to receive "the end of your faith, even the salvation of your souls" (1 Peter 1:3–5, 9).

If we find ourselves looking to heaven for the fulfillment of a promise, as the servant of Elijah looked toward the sea for a rain cloud (1 Kings 18:43), and we see nothing, we must not lose our confidence in God's promise or cease to pray for it. The promise and the word that goes forth from God's mouth will not return to Him void (Isa. 55:11, cf. 1 Kings 18:44). As William Spurstowe says: "The manner of the fulfilling of it may be various, but the performance of it is most certain. The blessing of the promise descends sometimes like rain in visible showers, producing the sensible effects of joy and peace in the soul; sometimes it falls like dew in a silent and imperceptible way...the virtue which it puts forth is real, but yet withal hidden and secret."[4]

We should remember, however, that many of God's promises are "*bonds of a different date,* meaning they are fulfilled in several ages and generations of the church, being so purposely ordered...that there might yet be a most plentiful reserve of new mercies unto the last ages

3. Ibid., 84.
4. Spurstowe, 82.

of the world."[5] How good God is to give His children such a store of promises that not only meet every one of our needs but also assure us that we can go to our graves rejoicing that His storehouse was not exhausted on us — an abundance of blessings and mercies will be left for our children and for the church that we love. God's mercies for those who follow us will be "new every morning" and to the end of the age.

Those promises that will be fulfilled in the future are also of great use to us in the present, for several reasons.[6] First, they support us during our present troubles. With the promises of future grace in hand, we are assured of our present safety. Spurstowe says: "The Church is as a ship… which may be tossed with tempests, but cannot be sunk and shipwrecked by them. It being the only heir of all the promises that God has made, it must live to enjoy them."[7] How can the church of God, the only rightful heir (under Christ) to God's promises, ever be destroyed as long as those promises remain to be inherited? Clearly, the church will survive to see every one of those promises fulfilled in its midst (Isa. 46:11b).

Second, the promises of future blessing are the bedrock of prayers that we make on behalf of the church. God has promised that Christ will reign until He has put all enemies under His feet (1 Cor. 15:25). In the meantime, the church shall "suck the milk of the Gentiles, and shalt suck the breast of kings" (Isa. 60:16). Do not these truths make us bold in seeking His face to remind Him of His gracious promises to His people? Spurstowe writes, "True it is, that the times and seasons when these things shall be, are unknown to [us]…but yet knowing that he who has promised, is faithful, [we] do with delight plead them in [our] prayers, and with faith embrace them in [our] arms."[8]

Third, these promises test the sincerity of a believer's affection and love for God's glory and the welfare of His church. Promises that offer us blessing in our afflictions tend to stir up earnestness in our prayers and consistency in our meditations. As Spurstowe reminds us, "But when a Christian can rejoice in such promises, which speak [of] the future

5. Ibid., 197.
6. Ibid., 198–205.
7. Ibid., 199.
8. Ibid., 202.

happiness of the Church when he is dead and gone; when it is sweet to him to think that Christ's throne shall hereafter be more exalted... it is an argument of a noble frame of heart, and of a spirit that is truly affected with the love of God's glory."[9]

Finally, the promises of future blessing comfort believers regarding their posterity. No concern is greater to believing parents than how their children will fare in their walk with Christ. The promises of future blessing and future stability for the church of Christ offer us unshakable hope. Spurstowe says: "Believers may comfortably hope, that what promises [they] themselves do fall short of, their posterity shall in one kind or other be partakers of. And though through the dark dispensations of present providences, the Church may seem to be in the midst of a howling wilderness, rather [than] near the borders of a *Canaan*, yet surely the Land of rest is not afar off, though it may to us be out of sight."[10]

The Problem of Delay

Despite the guarantee that God's promises have not been spoken to us in vain, we struggle when these promises appear to fall short of fulfillment. If the promises are ours as we belong to Christ, and if they will certainly be fulfilled upon us as He necessarily communicates them to His own, why do they sometimes appear to fail?

The reason for this is often a mystery to us. Still, we are not left without some understanding. In the wisdom of God, we live in a fallen world in which sin still has a place in God's sovereign plan. God's promises are held forth to us as a constant reminder that we are not to look to this world for life and fulfillment, but rather fix our gaze on the city whose designer and builder is God (Heb. 11:10). Let us therefore be convinced of what we have already established—the promises of God will be fulfilled because of the covenant foundation on which they are built and because the One to whom they belong is the Head of His body, the church. Just as oil poured on the head will run over the whole body and as a crown of blessing placed on the head will profit the whole

---

9. Ibid., 203.
10. Ibid., 205.

person, so the church will profit from every promise made to Christ by the Father.

Nevertheless, the Lord sometimes delays the accomplishment of His promises in our lives. According to Andrew Gray, God delays for the following reasons.[11] First, believers often grow in faith more during the delay of the fulfillment of a promise than after the accomplishment of it. For example, when David was pursued by Absalom, his actions were saintly and exemplary (2 Sam. 15:30; 16:11–12) while he was awaiting God's promise of return to his throne, but after David was restored, he fell into the sin of adultery with Bathsheba (2 Sam. 11:1–4). Experience teaches us that bearing our crosses in a sanctifying manner keeps us on our knees more than blessings, which often tempt us to self-dependence and self-indulgence.

Second, God delays the fulfillment of His promises to reveal and discipline us for our sloth. This is clear from the wanderings of Israel. The people of God wandered in the wilderness for forty years before seeing the fulfillment of the promise of entering the Promised Land, a result they could have obtained in a few days (Num. 14:33–34).

Third, God delays the accomplishment of promises so that we might exercise more faith. When the fulfillment of a promise is within reach, we lay hold of it with little effort. In that scenario, we are often tempted to reason that just as the promise's sweetness required little effort to obtain, so its fulfillment requires little faith. To prevent such false reasoning, the Lord often delays the fulfillment of a promise so that we might exercise more faith and be convinced anew that the blessings of God come to us only through lifelong faith in Christ (2 Cor. 1:20).

The fourth reason the Lord waits to fulfill a promise is to encourage us to pray more earnestly for the accomplishment of the promise. Gray says, "It is a bad improvement of delays, when we turn impatient; and…quit our confidence."[12] Instead, the delayed fulfillment of promises should compel us to pray. When Moses and Aaron met with the elders of Israel and told them of the Lord's promise of deliverance, they "believed:… then they bowed their heads and worshipped" (Ex. 4:31).

---

11. Gray, 120–21.
12. Ibid., 121.

Likewise, when the Lord promised to establish His covenant with David and his offspring forever, David turned to the Lord in prayer, saying, "Therefore hath thy servant found in his heart to pray this prayer unto thee" (2 Sam. 7:27). Later, David cried out to God, saying, "Remember the word unto thy servant, upon which thou hast caused me to hope" (Ps. 119:49).

Fifth, the Lord sometimes waits to fulfill a promise so that it might be sweeter when it is accomplished. Solomon admitted the ache of a deferred hope, but he also understood the greater sweetness of its fulfillment. He said, "Hope deferred maketh the heart sick: but when the desire cometh, it is a tree of life" (Prov. 13:12).

Sixth, the Lord often delays so we might be more dependent on Him. "Would you know what brings a Christian oftenest to God?" Gray asks. "It is a principle of necessity; and believe it, that if necessity did not drive a Christian unto the foot of the throne, he would seldom go from a principle of love, or from a principle of faith."[13] What mercy and love lie behind the Lord's delays, when they result in keeping us near the throne and dependent on Him!

Finally, the Lord sometimes delays so that the glory of His wisdom and power might appear brighter in the fulfillment of His promises. How often do we stand on the precipice of a promise that is about to be fulfilled and, viewing the landscape all around, confess that the Lord's timing was perfect? Likewise, do we not magnify His almighty power when His promises come to pass at a time so far removed from their inception that we have given up hope and even forgotten His Word? A promise delayed is not a sign of God's failing Word but rather a sign of God's wise providence, sovereign power, and sanctifying work.

A most important reason that God waits to fulfill some promises is our defective faith. Once again, Gray is helpful here.[14] He lists five defects in our faith toward God's promises:

- Our faith is often impatient and sluggish, failing to imitate "them who through faith and patience inherit the promises" (Heb. 6:12).

---

13. Ibid.
14. Ibid., 122–23.

- Our faith is inconsistent toward the promises, reading them one time as savory meat (Ex. 4:31) and other times as unsavory as the white of an egg (Ex. 6:9). The Lord has not changed and neither has His Word, but our inconstancy plagues us and distances us from the promises.

- We are not diligent in faith and prayer for the fulfillment of a promise, and in meditation for its lively nectar. Prayer and meditation strengthen our faith and set our hearts on the Word of God. We neglect these means to our peril.

- We build our faith more on what we see than on what is promised. When our circumstances affirm the promises of God, we believe, but when they are contrary to the promises, we reject confidence and hope. Gray does not speak unrealistically here; he admits that it is hard for a Christian to believe the Word of God when circumstances seem to declare that such a bold word from heaven will not be accomplished in his life. But however difficult it may be, we must take the apparent impossibility in one hand and the word of promise in the other and cry before the Lord: "O precious Christ, reconcile these two together, that impossibilities do not destroy the promise, but that the promise may be accomplished, notwithstanding this which I see before me."

- Our faith in the promises is not specific. We believe the general truth of God's promises, but we do not study His Word to make particular application of them.

As Gray says: "We ought not to limit infinite wisdom, nor to say to him that is infinite in strength, how can such a thing be? But answer all objections of misbelief with this—God has spoken it, and he will also do it."[15] May God strengthen our faith in His Word and cause His will to be accomplished in us. We trust He will do this, for "faithful is he that calleth you, who also will do it" (1 Thess. 5:24).

A Call to Faith

We began this chapter by asking to whom the promises of God rightly belong. Seeing that they rightly belong only to those who belong to Christ, the Lord Treasurer and Lord Keeper of the promises, we con-

---

15. Ibid., 168.

cluded that the promises are excluded from the wicked so long as they refuse to repent and embrace them. Though the accomplishment of a promise to a believer may be delayed, its fulfillment is sure. Indeed, though our faith is weak, God's promises to us will not ultimately fail, because Christ will bring His work in us to completion (Phil. 1:6; John 6:40; Eph. 5:25–27).

What can be done for those who are as yet excluded from this rich store of God in Christ? Only one thing: we must at all costs urge them to turn from their sin and to close with Christ, for "as we cannot come to Christ without the aid of a promise, so [we may] not rest in the promise without closing with Christ."[16]

For those of you who do not know Christ as Lord and Savior, we urge you to trust in Christ and His promises by considering that He is incomparably willing to receive you. Though your wickedness is great, your hardness adamant, your distance from grace far, yet He is so willing to have you that He *commands* you to come to Him. Hear Him say, "Come unto me, all ye that labour and are heavy laden, and I will give you rest" (Matt. 11:28); "Ho, every one that thirsteth, come ye to the waters, and he that hath no money; come ye, buy, and eat; yea, come, buy wine and milk without money and without price" (Isa. 55:1). All the objections you might summon as to why you cannot come to Christ can be cut in two with this knife: *This is His commandment.*[17]

If you refuse to come, consider that Christ will not forever endure such self-destructive madness. In Matthew 23:37, Jesus wept when He thought of Jerusalem's failure to recognize Him, saying, "O Jerusalem, Jerusalem…how often would I have gathered thy children together even as a hen gathers her brood under her wings, and ye would not!" Yet Jesus did not endure Jerusalem's self-destructive madness. By 70 A.D., Jerusalem was left desolate, having been destroyed by the Romans under the command of Titus.

Consider, too, how Christ, in great condescending love, invites you: "Look unto me, and be ye saved…for I am God, and there is none else" (Isa. 45:22). Note that you can have Christ by merely turning to look at

---

16. Spurstowe, 46.
17. Gray, 142.

Him, trusting fully in His promise! We may say it is impossible for our wicked eyes to look on Christ for salvation, but He has promised us a spirit of grace and prayer so that we may look on Him and be saved (Zech. 12:10).

Christ is so willing to have you that though He commands you to come and buy, He will freely give Himself to you. As Gray says, "Christ is both the seller...the ware, and...the buyer. Christ presents himself unto your hearts, and he desires to sell himself, and he persuades, and freely enables you to buy him. I will tell you what Christ does, he stands without our hearts, and within our hearts; he stands without, and knocks by the Word, and he stands within, and opens by his Spirit. Christ both commands and obeys, both within doors and without doors, and all this he does freely."[18]

Do you yearn to have the promises of God bequeathed to you? Then come to Christ; repent before Him and believe in Him as Savior, as Lord, and as *the* Promise of God. Do you lack sorrow for sin and faith in the Savior? Then come to Christ, for He promises to give what He commands and to supply what He requires (Acts 5:31). Both sorrow for sin (Acts 11:18) and saving faith (Acts 16:14) are *His* gifts that He promises to bestow on coming sinners. Therefore, let Christ's rich store of grace and forgiveness and His incomparable willingness to have you compel you to come to Him and be saved, for He has promised that "him that cometh to me I will in no wise cast out" (John 6:37). As sure as all the promises of the everlasting covenant are *Yes* and *Amen* for those who trust Christ, so shall the curses of this covenant be laid on those who refuse Christ.[19] Spurstowe concludes, "How inexcusable must be the neglect of those who do not with answerable hearts and desires embrace such precious offers."[20]

Christ our Savior promises, "Behold, I come quickly." So let the one who hears Him say, "Come," and turn to Him. "And whosever will, let him take the water of life freely" (Rev. 22:12, 17).

---

18. Ibid.
19. Ibid., 134.
20. Spurstowe, 245.

Study Questions

1. To whom does God bequeath His promises? Why?

2. William Spurstowe said God's promises are like a bag of gold coins: God unties the string and pours out the entire bag at believers' feet, saying, "Take what you will." If you are a believer, why do all of God's promises belong to you?

3. Though believers possess all of God's promises, they experience the reality of certain promises more than others. What promises of God have been particularly powerful in your life? What was happening to you when those promises were made precious to you? Why does God often tie together the preciousness of His promises and the greatness of our need?

4. Why are unbelievers excluded from receiving comfort from God's promises?

5. Read 1 Kings 18:41–46. How do these verses teach us to persevere in waiting for the fulfillment of God's promises? What should you do when you feel like God's promises are moving away from rather than toward fulfillment?

6. How can God have an inexhaustible supply of promises ready for His people at all times?

7. Spurstowe wrote: "The Church is as a ship...which may be tossed with tempests, but cannot be sunk and shipwrecked by them. It being the only heir of all the promises that God has made, it must live to enjoy them." What truth is Spurstowe emphasizing here? Are you enjoying God's promises? If not, why not?

8. Study 1 Corinthians 15:25. How do God's promises of future blessing serve as the bedrock of our prayers?

9. A relative has cancer and is undergoing heavy afflictions, including much pain. He is angry at God and rebuffs every attempt to point him to God's promises. Finally, he blurts out in frustration, "I've tried praying for a long time, and God never seems to answer. If God is as gracious as you say He is, why does He always delay in answering my prayers?" How would you respond?

10. How can we use the promises of God to call unbelievers to faith?

The Properties or Characteristics of God's Promises

Having strongly urged you to believe God's promises and to embrace Christ as God's Promise, we now turn to an examination of several characteristics of the promises. By the Spirit's grace, a study of these characteristics may activate your faith and bolster your assurance. The promises of God are distinguished by at least four characteristics: their freeness, fullness, firmness, and faithfulness.

The Free Promises of God

When Edward Leigh says that God's promises are free, he means they are undeserved. God does not give them to us because of any merit in us; rather, they proceed from His free favor and benevolence alone.[1] The apostle Paul makes this clear in Romans 4:16: "Therefore it is of faith, that it might be by grace; to the end the promise might be sure to all the seed; not to that only which is of the law, but to that also, which is of the faith of Abraham." The promise of the covenant of grace and all of the promises built upon it come to us as free and undeserved gifts through the righteousness of faith. God does not consider our merit in the giving of the promises because as creatures (not to mention as sinners) we have no merit before Him. Thus, William Spurstowe says, the promises "are not made to such as *deserve* mercy, but to such as *want* it; not to righteous persons, but to sinners, not to the whole, but to the sick."[2]

---

1. Leigh, 48.
2. Spurstowe, 50.

The promises "are all patents of grace, not bills of debt; expressions of love, not rewards of services; gifts, not wages," Spurstowe continues. "He that made many out of mercy might without the least umbrage of injustice have made none. Though his truth does tie him to the performance of them, yet his love and mercy only did move him to the making of them."[3] Bound up within the nature of a promise is its freeness. It must be given, for it cannot be earned. As Leigh says, "In ordinary speech we are said to make promises, but all God's promises are given (2 Pet. 1:4)."[4]

If we try to argue that God chose us to inherit His promises because of our number, Deuteronomy 7:7–8 says, "The LORD did not set his love upon you, nor choose you, because ye were more in number than any people; for ye were the fewest of all people: but because the LORD loved you, and because he would keep the oath which he had sworn unto your fathers, hath the LORD brought you out with a mighty hand, and redeemed you out of the house of bondmen, from the hand of Pharaoh king of Egypt." In other words, the Lord set His covenant love on us for no reason except that He loved us. Leigh says this truth "excellently sets forth the ground of God's love to rest altogether, in himself, and in his own good pleasure," since it excludes anything in us. Thus, we are heirs of the covenant, which is a "bundle of all the promises"[5] given to us solely by the free grace of God.

If we suggest that God's promises are ours because of our beauty, here, too, we are mistaken. Ezekiel 16:6–8 says, "And when I passed by thee, and saw thee polluted in thine own blood, I said unto thee when thou was in thy blood, Live;... I have caused thee to multiply as the bud of the field...and I spread my skirt over thee, and covered thy nakedness: yea, I sware unto thee, and entered into a covenant with thee, said the Lord GOD, and thou becamest mine." The prophet reflects here on Israel's beginnings, using graphic images to make clear the "naturally helpless, unpromising, and polluted condition of Israel"[6] when the

---

3. Ibid., 47.
4. Leigh, 48.
5. Ibid., 103. Cf. chap. 2 above.
6. Patrick Fairbairn, *An Exposition of Ezekiel* (Grand Rapids: Zondervan, 1960), 163.

Lord set His love on her. Thus, the promises of the covenant came to us when we were unlovely "in our blood" and undesirable, being naturally depraved and sinful.

Unable to argue our merit for the promises because of our number or beauty, we might still suggest that we have an *acquired* beauty or an acquired *righteousness* by which we deserve the benefit of God's promises. But even this cannot be defended. Titus 3:4–7 says, "But after that the kindness and love of God our Saviour toward man appeared, not by works of righteousness which we have done, but according to his mercy he saved us, by the washing of regeneration, and renewing of the Holy Ghost; which he shed on us abundantly through Jesus Christ our Saviour; that being justified by his grace, we should be made heirs according to the hope of eternal life." Truly, we are left with no ground in or about ourselves to claim as a basis for the Lord's grace. Our lack of merit stands out glaringly on every front, because there is nothing else to note.

Spurstowe seeks to bolster our confidence in the freeness of God's promises by saying:

> Were the way which leads to heaven a *ladder of duties*, and not a *golden chain of free grace*, I could not but fear, that the higher I climb, the greater would my fall prove to be; every service being like a brittle [rung] that can bear no weight; and the whole frame and series of duties at the best, far short of the ladder in *Jacob's* vision.... But the whole way of salvation from first to last, is all of mere grace, *that the promise might be sure* (Rom. 4:16). Every link of the golden chain is made up of free mercy.... And therefore I can challenge nothing of right, yet I may ask every thing of mercy, especially being invited by him who feeds not his people with empty promises, but gives liberally unto every one that asks, and upbraids not, either with former sins, or present failings (James 1:5).[7]

The glory of God's grace to us is unmistakable in its freeness. His motives are in His own bosom, by which He sovereignly chose to favor us with His promises. The first and great promise God gave to Adam after he had sinned (Gen. 3:15) was of God's free grace, and so too are all of the other evangelical promises, since they stand on the promise of

---

7. Spurstowe, 51–52.

Christ, in whom all the promises of God find their yes and amen (2 Cor. 1:20). To assure us of their freedom, Andrew Gray urges us to "consider and take up the infinite fulness and all-sufficiency of the Promiser, that there is nothing [outside] himself that can persuade him to give such promises."[8] The promises are the products of God's grace, not of any merit in us.

No unworthiness, therefore, should hinder us from believing or receiving the promises of God, since they are freely given to those who do not deserve them. We have the promise of John 6:37 that the Lord will receive us as we are—base, sinful, poor, and of no account—and will not cast us away.[9] Our unworthiness, then, rather than disqualifying us, actually qualifies us, for God has made His promises not to those who deserve grace but to those who need it (Matt. 11:28).[10] This truth does not discourage us from believing or quench our assurance, but rather inflames our assurance and stirs up our faith. Citing 2 Peter 1:4, Gray concludes, "To prove that the promises are gifts, I can bring no other argument so strong as this—*they are given to us.*"[11]

The Full Promises of God

The second characteristic of God's promises is their generosity with respect to both people and things. With respect to people, Leigh says we find three marks of fullness:

First, the promises are set forth in general to all, with such terms as *everyone*, *whoever*, *all*, and *anyone*. For example, John 3:16 says, "For God so loved the world, that he gave his only begotten Son, that whosoever believeth in him should not perish, but have everlasting life." Matthew 11:28 says, "Come to me, all ye that labour and are heavy laden, and I will give you rest." Revelation 22:17 says: "And let him that heareth say, Come. And let him that is athirst come. And whosoever will, let him take the water of life freely." Isaiah 55:1 says, "Ho, every

---

8. Gray, 137.
9. Leigh, 52.
10. Ibid.
11. Gray, 137.

one that thirsteth, come ye to the waters, and he that hath no money; come ye, buy, and eat; yea, come, buy wine and milk without money and without price." Acts 10:43 says, "To him give all the prophets witness, that through his name whosoever believeth in him shall receive remission of sins." John 7:37 states, "Jesus stood and cried, saying, If any man thirst, let him come unto me, and drink." John 6:37 says, "All that the Father giveth me shall come to me; and him that cometh to me I will in no wise cast out." John 6:40 says, "And this is the will of him that sent me, that every one which seeth the Son, and believeth on him, may have everlasting life: and I will raise him up at the last day." John 5:24 asserts, "Verily, verily, I say unto you, He that heareth my word, and believeth on him that sent me, hath everlasting life, and shall not come into condemnation; but is passed from death unto life." John 11:26 proclaims, "And whosoever liveth and believeth in me shall never die." And 1 John 2:1 says, "My little children, these things write I unto you, that ye sin not. And if any man sin, we have an advocate with the Father, Jesus Christ the righteous."

Second, the promises are offered to all sorts of people. Leigh says, "No sort of men are excluded, but in Christ they may have their part in these promises."[12] Luke 2:10 announces, "Fear not: for, behold, I bring you good tidings of great joy, which shall be to all people." Psalm 115:13 says, "He will bless them that fear the LORD, both small and great." Romans 10:12 declares, "For there is no difference between the Jew and the Greek: for the same Lord over all is rich unto all that call upon him." And Acts 10:35 says, "But in every nation he that feareth him, and worketh righteousness, is accepted with him."

Third, the promises are proclaimed indiscriminately to all together with the commandment to believe (e.g., Acts 2:38–39; 13:38–39; 16:30–34). God invites all to profit from His promises, but He also commands all to believe so they *can* profit (Acts 17:30–31). This shows that when the promises are not enjoyed, faith is lacking. How blessed, then, is the grace of the covenant by which God grants to His people the power, even the faith, to believe the promises (Ps. 110:3a; Acts 5:31; 11:18; 13:48; 16:14–15)!

---

12. Leigh, 54.

The fullness of God's promises can also be seen in the things that God has promised. Consider the largesse of the following verses: "No good thing will he withhold from them that walk uprightly" (Ps. 84:11); "Delight thyself also in the LORD; and he shall give thee the desires of thine heart" (Ps. 37:4); "Blessed is every one that feareth the LORD; that walketh in his ways. For thou shalt eat the labour of thine hands: happy shalt thou be, and it shall be well with thee" (Ps. 128:1–2); "And it shall come to pass, if thou shalt hearken diligently unto the voice of the LORD thy God…the LORD thy God will set thee on high above all nations of the earth: and all these blessings shall come on thee, and overtake thee…. And the LORD shall make thee the head, and not the tail; and thou shalt be above only, and thou shalt not be beneath" (Deut. 28:1–2, 13); and "But there the glorious LORD will be unto us a place of broad rivers and streams" (Isa. 33:21).

To those who fear God, the Lord has promised whatever is good for the soul, the body, the estate, the name, and the posterity. As Leigh says, "The promises in the Word extend themselves to all estates, to all conditions, and to all kinds of distresses whatsoever; they are a Christian's Catholicon [i.e., his universal remedy], being a help to all duties, a quickener of all graces, and a comfort in all troubles."[13]

Our tendency is to minimize the promises and to add to the precepts, but God has gone to great lengths to enlarge His promises so that no one is excluded but those who exclude themselves, Leigh says. Scripture says that *whoever* believes shall be saved. This means the "heinous sinner as well as the lesser; the poor beggar as well as the mightiest monarch, shall not perish, but have life eternal," if they believe.[14] The fullness of God's promises not only assures believers of salvation but also encourages all who hear of Christ to believe in Him.

However, let us warn the wicked who love to enlarge the promises and minimize the precepts to license their sin. They presume on God's pardon from His promise of salvation in Mark 16:16 to whoever believes and His promise of life in Ezekiel 18:21 to the sinner who repents. Leigh says these sweet promises are annexed to faith and repentance, but "out

---

13. Leigh, 56.
14. Ibid.

of these fragrant flowers, the wicked suck poison."[15] Presuming that it is easy to believe in Christ for salvation and to forsake one's sins and serve God with heart and body, the wicked, such as Agrippa and Felix, did thereby "out-slip" their day of grace. They will pay dearly for their presumption, for though true repentance is never too late, late repentance is seldom true repentance. Though God has promised pardon to the penitent, He has not promised repentance to the wicked.[16]

The Firm Promises of God

The third characteristic of God's promises is their firmness or stability. Every promise God gives will be fulfilled; therefore, not a single promise will disappoint a believer's hope and trust. The reason for this is the power of the One who gave these promises. All of God's promises are anchors for our faith because of the greatness of His power to fulfill them.

People often make promises that they are unable to fulfill, but God has infinite power to execute all His promises, whether small or great. Leigh says that while men promise mountains but deliver molehills, God promises His saints two whole worlds (this life and the life to come) and performs better than any.[17] He cannot be hindered by weakness, for that is a mark of the creature and not of the Creator (Pss. 115:3; 135:6; Dan. 4:34–35). Spurstowe says that while men's promises are subject to deficiency because of their lack of power and their inconstant will, "it is far otherwise with the promises of God, whose power no…impediments can arise to hinder, whose will no contingencies or emergencies can fall out to alter."[18]

Still, we are slow to believe in the limitlessness of God's power. According to Spurstowe, "the confining of God's power according to the narrow apprehensions and dwarfish thoughts that men naturally have of him in their hearts [is] the chief root of all that unbelief and

---

15. Ibid., 59.
16. Ibid.
17. Ibid., 77.
18. Spurstowe, 59.

distrust which is put forth in their lives (Ps. 78:19–20)."[19] God's Word is full of His promises to us, but when we are called upon to believe them, we measure their firmness by the improbabilities and impossibilities of our circumstances instead of the strength of God's power. Rather than looking upon ourselves as prisoners of hope with the promises of an all-powerful God in hand, we see ourselves as dead and dry bones in whom hope is lost (Ezek. 37:11). What a shame it is to waste away when the means of sustenance lies in our very hands! Let us, then, "have such conceptions of the power of God, as that whatever…impediments do arise between the promise and the fulfilling of it, though as high as mountains and as strong as the gates of hell, [they will be] by faith looked upon as difficulties which cannot check the power of God, but only magnify it."[20]

Consider Abraham. With good reason he is called the "father of the faithful," because he believed in the power of God to keep His promises though everything else spoke to the contrary. When God promised to give Abraham not only a son but a posterity as numerous as the stars of heaven (Gen. 15:4–5), everything seemed against him: he was too old to have children and Sarah's womb was barren. Yet the apostle Paul says in Romans 4 that Abraham "against hope believed in hope, that he might become the father of many nations, according to that which was spoken…. And being not weak in faith,… he staggered not at the promise of God through unbelief; but was strong in faith, giving glory to God; and being fully persuaded that, what he had promised, he was able also to perform" (vv. 18–21). Spurstowe explains it this way: "When nature afforded no grounds of hope or encouragement to confirm [Abraham's] expectation in the fulfilling of the promise, but suggested many posing arguments to impede and gainsay the truth of it and to make his faith as feeble as his body; yet [it was] then he exercised the fullness of assurance in believing and of hope in expecting the accomplishment of all that God had spoken."[21]

---

19. Ibid., 52–53.
20. Ibid., 54.
21. Ibid., 55.

Another example of Abraham's faith is seen in Genesis 22. God called Abraham to sacrifice his son, Isaac, through whom the promise of offspring was to come. Spurstowe says, "Though the stroke which Abraham's hand was stretched forth to give would not only have ended the life of his son, but also have cut off the promise at the very root… yet by the same eye of faith by which before he looked through a dead womb, he now looked through a bleeding sword unto the power of God, accounting that he was able to raise him up from the dead (Heb. 11:19)."[22] Abraham was so convinced of God's power and the stability of His promise that he believed God would sooner raise Isaac out of an ash heap than let one iota of His promise fall unfulfilled to the ground.

Our faith is not in the bare power of God, though this is enough to dispel all doubt, but in the relationship of this power to the promises. This power gives us as believers the stability on which we can firmly stand, no matter what buffets us. Our confidence is in God's strength to do what He has promised, despite any difficulties and temptations we may face. The peace and serenity this truth affords is summarized by Spurstowe: "No *valley* of trouble will be to him without a *door* of hope, no barren *wilderness* without *Manna*, no dry *rock* without *water*, no *dungeon* without *light*, no fiery *trial* without *comfort*, because he has the same Word and the same God to trust unto, whose power opened the sea as a door to be a passage from *Egypt* to *Canaan*, who led Israel in the desert with bread from heaven and water from a rock, who filled *Peter's* prison with a shining light, who made the three children to walk to and fro amidst the fiery furnace with joy and safety."[23]

The Faithful Promises of God

The fourth attribute of God's many promises is faithfulness or immutability. As with the other characteristics, the faithfulness of the promises rests on the faithfulness of the One who makes them. In other words, He who is faithful and immutable has set His seal upon the promises so that they warrant the same faithfulness and immutability as God Himself.

---

22. Ibid., 56.
23. Ibid., 57.

This faithfulness is based first of all on God's truthfulness. The One who has promised will be faithful to fulfill what He has promised because He is true to His Word and true to the covenant by which He has bound Himself to us and upon which the promises are founded.

Leigh offers the following support for the faithfulness of God's promises: Psalm 31:5 exalts God (who made the promises) as the faithful God; Ephesians 1:13 refers to the gospel (by which God's promises are published) as the word of truth; Revelation 3:14 refers to Christ (who has declared and merited the promises for us) as the faithful and true witness, while John 14:6 refers to Christ as truth itself; and John 14:17 refers to the Holy Spirit (who seals the truth of the promises to our hearts and stirs up our hope in them) as the Spirit of truth.[24]

Gray adds: "Must not the promises be unchangeable, that are received and merited by the Son, who is truth himself, and the *faithful Witness*, and *Amen*? Must not the promises be unchangeable, that are applied by the Holy Ghost, who is *the Spirit of truth*? And must not the promises be unchangeable, that are made known to us by the gospel, which is *the word of truth*? Was there ever any who could leave that upon record of God, that he was unfaithful in the accomplishment of his promises?"[25] Surely God's faithfulness has always been magnified by His promises.

Second, this faithfulness is based on God's willful debt to us in the promises. When God makes a promise to us, He makes Himself our debtor; therefore, we may humbly sue for what He owes us by virtue of His promise. Spurstowe says that although God's free grace has made Him a Promiser, "his promise has made him a debtor."[26]

In Psalm 143:1, David cried out to God for mercy, asking to be heard according to God's *faithfulness* and *righteousness*. By what manner is God's righteousness made manifest in answering our pleas for mercy? Certainly not by any merit of ours, for God is indebted to no creature. This righteousness can pertain only to the manner in which God has willfully indebted Himself to the penitent in the covenant of grace and

---

24. Leigh, 58.
25. Gray, 148–49.
26. Spurstowe, 47.

therein promised to grant mercy when it is sought. Thus, 1 John 1:9 says, "If we confess our sins, he is faithful and just to forgive us our sins, and to cleanse us from all unrighteousness." First John 2:1 adds: "My little children, these things write I unto you, that ye sin not. And if any man sin, we have an advocate with the Father, Jesus Christ the righteous." God's faithfulness and justice are therefore evident in keeping His promises to us as Christ, the Righteous One, takes our suit to the throne in His own name. Also, by virtue of the righteousness which He acquired for us, Christ secured the fulfillment of God's promise for us and administers it to us. Thus, God's words are as deeds and His promises as performances.

Third, the faithfulness of God's promises is based on His fulfillment of the first promise concerning Christ in Genesis 3:15. In the words of Romans 8:32, we may say, "He that spared not his own Son, but delivered him up for us all, how shall he not with him also freely give us all things?" In other words, the promise of salvation, the promise of deliverance, the promise of provision, and even the promise of glory are all branches of that first promise of Christ. In sending Christ into the world, God granted the root of all promises. How, then, could a single promise fall short of fulfillment?

Satan wants us to believe that God will fail to keep His promises. Weak Christians are so prone to surrender to temptations and fears of divine desertions that at times they are ready to distrust God and His promises. But the devil is a liar, and our weak faith is a poor measure of the truth of God's Word, for God is always faithful and so are His promises. The words of Balaam express God's faithfulness in fulfilling His promises: "God is not a man, that he should lie; neither the son of man, that he should repent: hath he said, and shall he not do it? or hath he spoken, and shall he not make it good?" (Num. 23:19). God is faithful, and He upholds the faith of His people by adding an oath to His promises (Heb. 6:17), "wherein he pawns his being, life, righteousness, truth, mercy, [and] power to perform all that he has spoken."[27]

---

27. Ibid., 59.

Finally, God assures us of the faithfulness of His promises by reminding us of His faithfulness to His covenant with creation (Gen. 8:21–22). God assures His people that He will keep His promise of forever setting a son of David on the throne (fulfilled in Christ, David's greater Son, Acts 13:34; Rom. 1:3), saying that it is as certain as night will follow day, and day, night (Jer. 33:14–22). Verses 20–21 declare, "Thus saith the LORD, if ye can break my covenant of the day, and my covenant of the night, and that there should not be day and night in their season; then may also my covenant be broken with David my servant, that he should not have a son to reign upon his throne."[28]

In his fourth sermon on 2 Peter 1:4, Gray proposes several golden pillars on which the unchangeableness of the promises is built. They are: the omnipotence of God (2 Cor. 6:18); the wisdom and infinite counsel of God (2 Sam. 23:5; Heb. 6:17); the infinite love of God (Deut. 7:8); the unchangeableness of the promises (Ex. 3:14); the faithfulness of God, that He is One who cannot lie but will certainly make out what He has spoken; and the justice of God (1 John 1:9). Of this last pillar, Gray says: "The accomplishment of the promises is not only an act of love but also an act of justice. We confess, indeed, love and mercy makes the promises, but justice and truth also put God to the accomplishment of them."[29]

Leigh concludes: "Never could anyone tax God for promise breaking. God, as he doth out-vie all for the largeness of his promises, so is he unmatchable for faithfulness in fulfilling his promises."[30] Gray adds: "Dispute less, and believe more!—what profit shall you have of your disputings? And if you would produce all your strong arguments, why you should not believe the promises, you may drown them in this immense depth—*God is unchangeable.*"[31] Therefore, we should wait with patience for the fulfillment of God's promises, not limiting him to

---

28. See also Ps. 89:36–37; Jer. 31:35–36.
29. Gray, 149.
30. Leigh, 76.
31. Gray, 152.

time, manner, or means of accomplishment, for His servants have ever found Him better and never worse than His Word.[32]

What could possibly stand up against such inviting characteristics? What arguments could you possibly propose against the freedom, fullness, firmness, and faithfulness of God's promises? There are none. If pressed, you would undoubtedly come up empty-handed. However stalwart your lofty arguments might appear, their luster is only surface deep; they are like rotten posts painted over that are pleasant to the eye but worthless against a storm.

The brightness of these attributes attests their worth above all the wisdom of men, no matter what arguments men might thrust forth to defend themselves. Moreover, the glory of these divine attributes exposes our foolishness for what it is. These characteristics are indeed sufficient, and by the grace of God they draw forth our faith and ground our assurance in His promises.

It now remains to discuss how we may rightly use the promises of God. Let us turn to that topic now, following the Puritan method of instructing the mind and educating the understanding prior to offering application.

Study Questions

1. Explain how God's promises are both free and costly at the same time.

2. If you are saved, why did God choose you?

3. How should the freeness of God's promises strengthen our assurance of faith and bolster our confidence in God daily?

---

32. Ibid., 77–78.

4. To whom is the gospel offered? Prove your answer from Scripture. Who is excluded from the fullness of God's invitations to come to Christ and embrace His promises?

5. Read Acts 24 and Acts 26. How did Felix and Agrippa out-slip their day of grace? How does this serve as a warning for unbelievers today?

6. Read about Abraham's call to sacrifice his son in Genesis 22. How could Abraham be so convinced of God's promise that he believed God would sooner raise Isaac out of an ash heap than let one iota of His promise fall unfulfilled to the ground? How did Abraham demonstrate that faith?

7. In what ways are God's promises faithful and unchangeable? What should that teach us in this promise-breaking world?

8. Since Christians are called to reflect Christ's image in this world, we too must be faithful to our promises. Can you think of promises that you have made that you have not fulfilled? What three things should you do about those unfulfilled promises?

9. Too often we make promises lightly. For example, we tell people we will pray for them but then fail to engage in serious intercession on their behalf. How can we be more faithful in fulfilling our promises to pray for other Christians? What will help us to be more faithful in fulfilling promises that we make?

10. How do all of God's promises flow out of His first promise concerning Christ in Genesis 3:15? In what way is this comforting to you?

The Right Use of God's Promises

Lest we lose sight of the foundational nature of all that has gone before, let us briefly retrace our steps by outlining the truths we have come to understand and on which we can now stand.

First, the divine promises are declarations of God's goodwill toward us, and we are warranted, even commanded, to hope for, believe in, and solicit God for what they declare, whether temporal or eternal. The promises of God bridge the gap between His declaration and performance of good on our behalf, making them most precious and sweet as they bring us into possession of Christ, and with Him, all things that God has in store for His people.

Second, all of the divine promises, whatever their content, are built on the foundation of the covenant of grace and its mother promise that God will be our God and we will be His people. It is because of this relationship that God graciously establishes with us that we enjoy any fruit of His goodness. We are brought into this relationship with God by the saving work of His Spirit and on the basis of the atoning work of His Son, and it is within this relationship that God the Father in Christ freely gives us all things. Every promise is founded on the covenant of grace. Furthermore, Christ is the fountainhead from which all the promises flow to us; they have their yes and amen in Him, since every promise of God offers what rightly belongs to Him and what only He can give. Having Christ, we have everything, whereas outside of Christ, we have nothing. When we embrace the promise of Christ, we have God's entire store, with one hand stretched as far back as election and the other as far forward as the beatific vision. But if we reject Christ, be our hands ever so full and our arms stretched around the globe itself, we have nothing at all and will appear before God empty-handed.

Third, the promises of God belong only to those who, by grace, have been brought into union with Christ through faith and belong to Him. This excludes all who are outside of Christ and urges them to be united to Him so they might reap the benefit of God's goodness poured forth in His promises. While the promises are a comfort to the children of God, they prod all others, graciously pointing them to Christ, in whom they too might know God's goodness.

Fourth, the promises of God are free, given to us by His grace; full, inviting all people without partiality and promising them everything they need without limit; firm, founded on God's almighty power to fulfill; and faithful, resting on the immutability of Him who declared them. Such characteristics compel our faith and sustain our assurance.

With such beautiful ground behind us, what glory still lies ahead of us! It may be helpful to say here that this chapter's importance is its transitional character. As mentioned in the introduction to chapter one, the genius of Puritan methodology is its practice of addressing the mind through instruction before addressing the will through exhortation. Both mind and will must be addressed to change the whole person, but since the will can be moved to action only by the direction of the mind, the mind must first be instructed in what is good so that the will (presupposing God's grace) can in turn choose what is good. Our aim in the preceding four chapters has been to put forth instruction, drawing from three eminent Puritans. That sets the stage for what lies ahead of us, namely, exhortation in applying the promises to various concerns and challenges in our lives.

With that glorious end in view, we begin this chapter by addressing in a general way the right use of God's promises. If the promises are all that we have seen them to be, they are more useful to us in this world than the very air we breathe. If God is behind them as their support and in them as their essential matter, then we have no greater security on earth for heaven and no greater access to the full enjoyment of God than in the divine promises. If the promises of God are His hand of bounty to us, nothing is more essential in life than to know what they are and how to profit from them. Having seen what they are, let us now consider (though only briefly, so as not to rob the remaining chapters) how we as God's people are to use the promises that have been so freely given to us (2 Peter 1:3–4).

Edward Leigh begins his chapter on the right use of the promises by saying, "The right use of the promise is a means to sweeten all our afflictions, confirm our faith, excite us to well doing, and to breed contention of mind[1] in all estates and conditions whatsoever."[2] If such benefits come from rightly using the promises, we are compelled to ask what that involves. We suggest that rightly using the promises involves believing them, applying them (depending on them), and praying them.

These exhortations may seem superfluous in light of what was said in previous chapters, but they are not. How difficult it sometimes is to believe the Word of God; how forgetful we are to make real-life application of its teachings so as to depend on the Word when other props are on hand; and how averse are we to take up the promises of God in prayer! Such exhortations must be regularly set before us if we are to profit from God's promises.

We must believe the promises

Many of us know that the Scriptures are full of God's promises. Many of us can quote some of those promises if called upon to do so. Yet few of us really believe them, and few of us can testify about a time when the promises sweetened our bitter afflictions, confirmed our weak and faltering faith under trial, compelled us to duty in the face of adversity, or provided us with unexplainable contentment in a time of disruption and upheaval. Few of us know the consolation of Jeremiah, who, after lamenting God's judgment on Jerusalem, found lasting comfort in God's covenant promise. In Lamentations 3:21–23, the prophet says: "This I recall to my mind, therefore have I hope. It is of the LORD's mercies that we are not consumed, because his compassions fail not. They

---

1. I.e., contentment.
2. Leigh, 23–24.

are new every morning: great is thy faithfulness." We know God's promises are true and are given to us, but so often we fail in the elementary step of believing what God has promised, and therefore we fail to enjoy their fruits.

What the author of Hebrews said of Israel in the wilderness often describes our failure to believe God's promises: "For unto us was the gospel preached, as well as unto them: but the word preached did not profit them, not being mixed with faith in them that heard it" (Heb. 4:2). As Hebrews 3:19 says, "They could not enter in [to God's rest] because of unbelief." Had Israel believed, she would have enjoyed the substance of God's promises, namely, His rest.

Thus, we must cry out to God like the father of the boy with the unclean spirit: "I believe; help thou mine unbelief!" (Mark 9:24), knowing that as we do so, God will be as good to us as Christ was to that father. He will forgive our weak faith and work by His Spirit to increase our faith so that we will not fail to enjoy in Christ all that God has promised us. When faced with the promises of God, we will be "not of them who draw back unto perdition; but of them that believe to the saving of the soul" (Heb. 10:39).

The need for an active and vital faith in God's promises is described in 2 Peter 1:4, where we are told that it is through them, or through our believing them, that we become partakers of the divine nature and escape from the corruption that is in the world because of sinful desire. In other words, while being united to Christ and consecrated to God is a sovereign act of God upon us and not something we ourselves accomplish, it is still true, as Peter goes on to assert in verses 5–11, that we enjoy being in Christ and being separated unto Him in daily experience by appropriating this union and consecration through faith. In other words, while what we have is divinely given, we can enjoy it experientially only by faith. That faith is not mere assent but an embracing faith by which we cleave to the promises; it is a faith that welcomes the promises, clasps them, embraces them, and kisses them. When our hearts have such a grip on the promises of God, then, like Simeon, we indeed hold Christ in our arms (Luke 2:28).[3]

3. Ibid., 25–26.

Andrew Gray says the unspeakable gain that flows to a Christian through the promises is enjoyed through the act of believing them, for in believing the promises, the soul "rises unto a likeness and conformity to [Christ] in holiness, wisdom, and righteousness."[4] We cannot expect to experience Christ's blessings if we fail to sincerely believe what God has said. As Gray notes: "We must lay this for a ground, that the fruit of all comes to him through the believing of the promises, and in making application of them."[5]

Gray then describes the fruit of believing the promises.[6] He says, first, that believing the promises greatly promotes the difficult work of mortification. As 2 Corinthians 7:1 tells us, "Having therefore these promises, dearly beloved, let us cleanse ourselves from all filthiness of the flesh and spirit, perfecting holiness in the fear of God."

Second, believing the promises helps a Christian in the spiritual and heavenly performance of prayer. In 2 Samuel 7:27, when David received God's promise, he concluded, "Therefore hath thy servant found in his heart to pray this prayer unto thee." In Psalm 119:147, he says, "I prevented the dawning of the morning, and cried: I hoped in thy word."

Third, believing the promises upholds a Christian afflicted by spiritual desertions and temptations, for "faith will see a morning approaching in the time of the greatest trouble"[7] (cf. Pss. 94:18; 119:81).

Fourth, believing fosters patience and submission in the midst of the saddest afflictions. As David writes, "This is my comfort in my affliction: for thy word hath quickened me," and, "Unless thy law had been my delights, I should then have perished in mine affliction" (Ps. 119:50, 92).

Fifth, believing helps a Christian distance himself from the world and live more as a pilgrim on earth. Hebrews 11:13 tells us that the patriarchs died in faith, not having received the things promised but acknowledging the truth of them because the things promised were to

---

4. Gray, 158.
5. Ibid.
6. Ibid., 158–63.
7. Ibid., 160.

be found not on earth but in God (v. 16). They experienced the promises as "strangers and pilgrims on the earth."

Sixth, believing is the mother of much spiritual joy and divine consolation, and helps a Christian to express praise. David's hope in the promises moved him to say to the Lord, "But I will hope continually and will yet praise thee more and more" (Ps. 71:14). Peter talked of inexpressible joy because of what the promises say about Christ and the assurance that is ours as we hope in Him (1 Peter 1:8–9).

Seventh, believing is a notable means to attain spiritual life (Isa. 38:16; Ps. 119:50). Gray asks: "What is the great occasion that our hearts are oftentimes dying within us like a stone, and we are like unto those that are free among the dead? Is it not because we do not make use of the promises?"[8]

Eighth, believing raises a Christian's esteem of the thing promised. Gray asks, "Why do we write above the head of the great things of the everlasting covenant: This is a Zoar, a little one? Is it because we do not believe?" He continues, "If we had so much faith as a grain of mustard-seed, we would cry forth, 'How excellent are these things that are purchased to the saints and how eternally are they made up, that they have a right but to one line of the everlasting covenant, that is well ordered in all things, and sure.'"[9]

Ninth, belief is the door through which the accomplishment of the promises enters (Luke 1:45; Isa. 25:9). Gray says, "Faith makes our thoughts to ascend, and misbelief makes our thoughts descend, in relation to the mercies of heaven."[10]

Tenth, believing secures the advantages mentioned in 2 Peter 1:4: we are brought to the blessed conformity with God that we lost in the Fall and we put off the ugly defilements that are Satan's images on our souls because of the Fall.

How fruitful, then, is belief in the promises of God, and how barren is a life of unbelief! Not surprisingly, knowing that the great harvest comes by believing the promises, the devil feels compelled to strike at

---

8. Ibid., 162.
9. Ibid.
10. Ibid., 163.

our faith in the promises—not so much at our faith in the truth of them as at the faith by which we apply those promises to ourselves.[11]

Echoing Leigh and Gray, William Spurstowe cautions us not to rest in "a general faith, which goes no further than to give a naked assent unto the promises of the Gospel as true; but does not put forth itself to receive and embrace them as good." True faith is not merely an act of understanding but a work of the heart, as Romans 10:10 tells us, he says.[12] True faith yields assent to the truth of the promise so that it might draw near to Christ and embrace the fruit of the promise, casting itself on Him for life and happiness. Indeed, the danger of a mere assenting faith is seen in Simon Magus (Acts 8:13, 23), the multitudes who heard Christ (John 2:23), and the five foolish virgins (Matt. 25:11), each of whom believed God's promises were true but did not receive and embrace the promises as good.

How great is the distance between the assenting faith of devils (Matt. 8:29) and the trusting faith of true believers (Matt. 16:16), for one is bare credence while the other is divine affiance.[13] Scripture makes this clear in describing the trusting faith of true believers as rolling and staying upon God (Isa. 50:10), trusting in Him (Isa. 26:4), receiving Him (Col. 2:6), and coming unto Him (John 6:36), "all which expressions do speak the spiritual motions and affections of the heart towards Christ in cleaving and adhering unto him, which believers only exercise."[14]

By contrast, unbelievers (often portrayed as hypocrites and castaways) do not rely on God or look to Him (Isa. 31:1), do not trust in Him (Ps. 78:22), do not receive Christ (John 1:11), and do not come to Him (John 5:40), for their faith is merely "a form of faith, [lacking] the power and efficacy which accompanies saving faith."[15]

Christ and His promises do not benefit anyone but those who make a particular application of both Christ and the promises to themselves, an application made by believing.[16] Whoever looks for "the real

---

11. Leigh, 31.
12. Spurstowe, 111.
13. Ibid., 113.
14. Ibid., 114.
15. Ibid.
16. Ibid., 115.

enjoyment of comfort and peace from the promises, [must not] please themselves in a general assent, which is little worth; but must endeavor to clear and evidence their peculiar interest in Christ and his promises, by a [trusting] application of them unto themselves."[17]

Let us, then, believe the promises of God, not merely assenting to their truthfulness, but trusting in their goodness and just application unto us in our estate, for "Christ would account it an excellent courtesy, that you should not dispute, but believe; and that you would look upon your necessities, as his call to believe the promises."[18]

We must apply the promises

Application of the promises, in brief, means that we do not sit idle and wait for the promises of God to come true in our lives, but rather, by the Spirit's grace, we lean on them as the king of Israel leaned on his captain's hand (2 Kings 7:2), resort to them as David resorted to the stone in his pouch (1 Sam. 17:40), and eye them as Elijah's servant eyed the sea, waiting for the rain cloud (1 Kings 18:43–44).

We lean on the promises as the king leaned on his captain's hand by serious and frequent meditation upon them. In other words, we make the promises our constant support so that we might "draw forth the sweetness and discover the beauty"[19] within them. Do we expect to empty a well by drawing a single bucketful or mine a river of all its gold by washing a single panful of water and soil? Neither should we expect to empty a promise of all its worth, comfort, consolation, encouragement, and assurance with a cursory look at it or a rote recital of it. Spurstowe says meditation on a particular promise is like looking at the night sky.[20] At first, we see one or two stars that seem to be struggling to reach us with their light. As we look again, those same stars put forth a brightness that not only lights up their space in the sky but also enables us to see other stars that we could not see at first. Finally, when

---

17. Ibid., 120–21.
18. Gray, 128.
19. Spurstowe, 78.
20. Ibid.

we look once more, the light of those stars seems to so increase that the whole sky appears to be standing at attention as innumerable stars shine in every quarter.

In application, Spurstowe writes, "When a Christian first turns his thoughts towards the promises, the appearances of light and comfort which shine from them do oft-times seem to be as weak and imperfect rays which neither scatter fears nor darkness; [but] when again he sets himself to ripen and improve his thoughts upon them, then the evidence and comfort which they yield to the soul, is both more clear and distinct; but when the heart and affections are fully fixed in the meditation of a promise, Oh! what a bright mirror is the promise then to the eye of faith! What legions of beauties do then appear from every part of it which both ravish and fill the soul of a believer with delight!"[21]

Our problem, then, is not so much a lack of faith but a failure to truly apply the promises, so as to depend on them. As we read the Scriptures and come across a particular promise that directly speaks to our situation, we yield a hearty amen to it, but then we quickly close our minds as we close our Bibles and think no more of it, trying once again to live independently from the promises. It is as if we expect the fulfillment of a promise to drop from the sky into our laps simply by our knowing and assenting to it. When the fulfillment of that promise does not happen, we look for another promise, hoping to light upon one with efficacy.

The problem is not the promise; it is our failure to lean and depend on it in meditation, to confer with it and chew on it until we feel the sweetness of it in our mouths. It is by meditation that we "dive into the depths of the promise" and "make clefts into the promise."[22] For as Spurstowe says, "One promise thoroughly ruminated and mediated upon is like a morsel of meat well chewed and digested, which distributes more nourishment and strength to the body than great quantities taken down whole."[23] Applying the promises of God means fixing our minds on them

---

21. Ibid., 78–79.
22. Ibid., 80.
23. Ibid., 79.

until the very weight and number of our thoughts, like a winepress, turn the promise into "a strengthening and reviving cordial."[24]

Applying the promises also means resorting to them as young David resorted to the choice stone in his pouch in the midst of battle. It means always keeping some specific promises on hand. We may not know when the waters will rise around us, but if we are prepared, we can make our escape to higher ground. We may not know when pain will lay us low, but if we have medicine on hand, we can often quickly find relief. Likewise, we may be ignorant of the temptations we will face in a given day, the hardships that will befall us, the effect the economy will have on us, and the doubts that might arise in our minds. But why should we be caught unawares? Why should we wait until the trial comes before we seek relief? Applying the promises means keeping those that pertain to various trials "at the ready" so that, come what may, we have recourse to divine support and comfort.

Spurstowe suggests several promises that we might keep on hand. In times when we find ourselves burdened with sin and giving way to despair, we can reach for the stone of Exodus 34:6–7: "The LORD, the LORD God, merciful and gracious, longsuffering, and abundant in goodness and truth, keeping mercy for thousands, forgiving iniquity and transgression and sin, and that will by no means clear the guilty." If we are mourning a lack of holiness, we should reach for Hosea 14:5–7, in which God promises to plant and water all our graces: "I will be as the dew unto Israel: he shall grow as the lily, and cast forth his roots as Lebanon. His branches shall spread, and his beauty shall be as the olive tree, and his smell as Lebanon. They that dwell under his shadow shall return; they shall revive as the corn, and grow as the vine: the scent thereof shall be as the wine of Lebanon." Think of the encouragement and comfort we can draw from Isaiah 43:2–3 in times of danger: "When thou passest through the waters, I will be with thee; and through the rivers, they shall not overflow thee: when thou walkest through the fire, thou shalt not be burned; neither shall the flame kindle upon thee. For I am the LORD thy God, the Holy One of Israel, thy Saviour." God promises either to deliver

---

24. Ibid., 81.

us from troubles or to support us in the midst of troubles, but in either case we have great comfort with such a promise on hand.

As authors, we witnessed this first hand only weeks after these words were written. We were called to co-pastor a dear middle-aged believer in London who had just been diagnosed with cancer even as she was seeking grace to cope with two blind children with severe kidney promises, one of whom was only expected to live for a few weeks after our visit. When we asked, "How are you managing to cope with all these trials," she responded with a smile, and said, "The Lord has been so good to me. He keeps bringing back His precious promises into my mind—often in the night seasons—even promises that I had long forgotten. His promises are more than sufficient for all my trials."

How lost we are when we remain ignorant of the divine promises! We believe that we have recourse to them as the children of God, but we fail to remind ourselves of that. We neglect to keep them on hand as stones at the ready, and when a lion, a bear, or a Goliath approaches, we feel empty-handed and suffer the loss of available comfort and peace. As Spurstowe says, "Oh! how securely and contentedly then may a believer, who acts his faith in such promises, lay himself down in the bosom of the Almighty in the worst of all his extremities! Not much unlike the infant that sleeps in the arms of his tender mother with the breast in his mouth, from which, as soon as ever it wakes, it draws a fresh supply that satisfies his hunger, and prevents its unquietness."[25]

Finally, applying the promises means eyeing them as Elijah's servant eyed the sea in search of a rain cloud and waiting patiently for their fulfillment. Peter speaks of scoffers in the last days who mock the promise of Christ's Second Coming because "all things continue as they were from the beginning of the creation" (2 Peter 3:3–4). Because things do not materialize as expected and fulfillment is so long in coming, people accuse God of lying and give up on waiting. If we are to apply the promises, we must be patient, neither casting away our confidence in them nor neglecting to lean and depend on them daily for encouragement and hope. God has promised, "For as the rain cometh down,

25. Ibid., 95–96.

and the snow from heaven, and returneth not thither, but watereth the earth, and maketh it bring forth and bud…so shall my word be that goeth forth out of my mouth: it shall not return unto me void, but it shall accomplish that which I please, and it shall prosper in the thing whereto I sent it" (Isa. 55:10–11).

Spurstowe says we often act like sick people who conclude that medicine is unhelpful if it does not immediately remove their pain, when all the while the medicine is working to prevent the sickness from taking greater hold on their bodies. Even so, when we are in difficulty and the promises or ordinances of God offer no immediate relief, we grow impatient and are prone to throw off the use of such means, concluding that they are of no value.

The loss of faith in the promises is more devastating than can be imagined, for though we may not perceive what work God is doing in our hearts, and though we may not see the fruit that we expect to see, it always profits us to keep our eye on the promises of God. They have a cleansing and purifying effect on our souls, which we may not perceive but which manifests itself in keeping us from evil things and from stumbling into sin. Without the quiet and insensible work of the promises in our hearts, we might be led far astray. As Spurstowe puts it, "And so may I say to them that complain [that] they ruminate often upon the promises in their thoughts, plead them in their prayers, read them in the Word, but yet find no benefit or fruit from them; that in so doing, they are not only more holy and free from lusts than others who neglect them; but far better than otherwise [they] themselves would be, should they not be employed in such spiritual and blessed services."[26] Sometimes the promises fall like spring showers in the middle of the day, and at other times they light upon us as imperceptibly as the dew during the night hours. In the latter case, the virtue of their activity is as real as in the former.

Our hope in eyeing the promises is that their fulfillment will indeed come. Habakkuk 2:3 encourages us not to lose heart but to wait for the Lord. He says, "Though it tarry, wait for it; because it will surely come,

---

26. Ibid., 85.

it will not tarry." The Lord has set a date and time for the fruition of His promises, but that is His timing, not ours. We must look to Him as the all-wise God and wait on Him with submission and contentment, for His timing is perfect; He is never late but is always on time. Spurstowe says, "A good heart, though it will not let God wait long…for its obedience, yet it will wait as long as God sees good for his promises, saying only with David, Remember the word unto thy servant, upon which thou hast caused me to hope" (Ps. 119:49).[27] Indeed, we must remember that "promises are not made and fulfilled at the same time, no more than sowing and reaping are on the same day."[28]

Gray says we must wait on God's timing and not give up confidence when what we sense does not agree with what is promised. He says our sense is not part of the promise; rather, it is an indulgence that the Lord dispenses as He sees fit. In other words, when God promises something, He does not promise that sense and reason will precede or accompany the fulfillment. We must not judge the probability or certainty of a promise being fulfilled upon these grounds. Gray says: "Do not expect sensible comforts immediately after you have believed the promises. A Christian may apply the promises and yet want the joy and sweetness that is in them."[29]

David cries out for God to fulfill His Word: "My soul cleaveth unto the dust: quicken thou me according to thy word" (Ps. 119:25). Gray explains: "I would press this upon you—prophesy nothing before your believing of the promise; but having believed, you may surely prophesy that the promise shall be accomplished in its own time, and the word that he has spoken shall certainly come to pass. But as for sense, as for quickening, as for comforting, as for receiving, you must put a blank in the hand of Christ, to dispense these things to you as he sees fit."[30]

Furthermore, Gray says, those promises that are fulfilled after much faith and a long wait are more precious and sweet because we have spent many nights in the watchtower with our eyes on the horizon. In a sense,

---

27. Ibid., 89.
28. Ibid., 63.
29. Gray, 130.
30. Ibid.

they have cost us much; therefore, we prize them when they come. If we cast off hope, though we may eventually see the fulfillment of a promise, it will not be as sweet to us as it would have been had we continued to watch for it. Gray concludes, "I think sometimes a Christian is like that misbelieving lord in 2 Kings 7:2, that though he meets with the accomplishment of a promise, yet he does not taste of the sweetness that is in it, because he did not believe the word of the Lord."[31]

Let us, then, who believe the promises of God go on to apply them to ourselves through serious meditation on them and habitual recourse to them. Let us patiently wait for their fulfillment, thereby preparing ourselves to take possession of and enjoy the full sweetness of them when, in the Lord's wise timing and way, they are fulfilled unto us.

We must pray the promises

Praying the promises is the most important element in the right use of the promises. This is because, despite all our striving to believe and apply the promises of God, we sometimes still find ourselves "troubled on every side; without [are] fightings, within [are] fears" (2 Cor. 7:5), and "pressed out of measure, above strength, insomuch that we [despair] even of life," feeling that "we [have] the sentence of death in ourselves" (2 Cor. 1:8–9). Are we then without hope? When we find ourselves in such dire straits, are we destined to be tossed on the waves of life's storms without the anchor of divine promises?

Not at all. As distant and out of reach as the promises of God may seem to us in such straits, a mighty means of comfort is still available to us. That means is prayer. Even when everything seems to have failed and the very bottom of life seems to have fallen out, if we but cry out to God in prayer, even if we merely utter groans before the throne of God (Ps. 22:11–15), it will be enough. We will find almost unexplainable strength to go on, we will find hope for another day, and we will be enabled to boast of the Lord and His promises (Ps. 22:19, 22–24). Prayer, more than anything else, denies self, relinquishes control, con-

---

31. Ibid., 166.

fesses need, leans on God, goes outside of ourselves, and cries out for help. Prayer that is founded on the promises of God and puts Him in remembrance of them will more than make up for the deficit of our unbelief, impatience, and doubt. Prayer that pleads the promises of God and confesses our hope in His Word will never disappoint, but will strengthen us and carry us through the valley of the shadow of death until the Lord grants relief (Pss. 27:12–14; 21:7).

Praying the promises, according to Leigh, means two things: using them as the ground for what we ask and as the rule for how we ask it.

The promise of God for a certain blessing gives us a sure ground on which to plead for that blessing. "We must see the things we ask, made ours in some promise and engagement, before we presume to ask them,"[32] Leigh says. Without that ground, we have no hope of being heard, for as the apostle says in 1 John 5:14–15, "And this is the confidence that we have in him, that, if we ask any thing according to his will, he heareth us: and if we know that he hear us, whatsoever we ask, we know that we have the petitions that we desired of him." To ask in faith, believing that we are heard and will certainly be answered, is nothing other than pleading upon a particular promise. Leigh concludes, "Therefore he that prays without a promise, denies his own request,"[33] for "to pray in faith is to go as far as the promise goes."[34] Gray says belief in the promises is a great help to a Christian in his prayers because "a Christian that believes the promises can take the promise in his hand and present it unto God, and say, 'Fulfill this promise, since thou wilt not deny thy name, but art faithful.'"[35]

Several saints mentioned in the Scriptures did just that. Jacob was afraid that Esau his brother might kill him, so he called on God by pleading His promise (Gen. 32:9–12). Before crossing the Jabbok River, Jacob prayed, "Deliver me, I pray thee, from the hand of my brother, from the hand of Esau: for I fear him, lest he will come and smite me, and the mother with the children. And thou saidst, I will surely do thee

---

32. Leigh, 39.
33. Ibid., 40.
34. Ibid., 41.
35. Gray, 160.

good, and make thy seed as the sand of the sea, which cannot be numbered for multitude" (vv. 11–12).

Daniel also pleaded a promise of God in prayer. Daniel 9:2–3 says: "I Daniel understood by books the number of the years, whereof the word of the LORD came to Jeremiah the prophet, that he would accomplish seventy years in the desolations of Jerusalem. And I set my face unto the Lord God, to seek by prayer and supplications, with fasting, and sackcloth, and ashes." He then prayed that God would deliver His people as He had promised to do (vv. 4–19).

Likewise, David asked the Lord to bless his house on the basis of the Lord's prior promise to do that very thing (2 Sam. 7:28–29). Such prayers of faith have a particular promise of God as their object and call on the Lord to do as He has said.[36]

Does this mean we cannot pray in faith for things we may desire but for which have no particular promise from the Lord? Leigh anticipates this question by asking: "If I pray for the salvation of another, I have no promise,[37] so how then can I pray in faith? So likewise when a man prays to be guided in business, to have such an enterprise to be brought to pass, to have deliverance from such a trouble, such a sickness or calamity that he lies under, he finds no particular promise, and for aught he knows, it shall never be granted: how can he be said to pray in faith? For to pray in faith is to believe that the thing shall be done."[38]

Leigh's answer to his own question brings us back to the goodness and wisdom of God, reminding us that whether or not we have a promise to plead, faith involves our trust and submission. Leigh says: "To pray in faith is to go as far as the promise goes. Now no particular man has any particular promise, that he shall have such a deliverance, that he shall have such a mercy granted him; and therefore it is not required to believe, that that particular thing should be done, but [rather] that God is ready to do that which is best for me, in such a particular, that which shall be most for his own glory, and my good."[39] We may still pray in

---

36. See also Neh. 1:8–11 and 2 Chron. 20:1–12.
37. I.e., a promise that that *particular person* for whom we pray will indeed be saved.
38. Leigh, 40.
39. Ibid., 41.

faith, but in the faith of submission and not with definite assurance. In this type of faith, we believe we will receive an answer of good tidings, knowing that the good we receive will be determined according to what most glorifies the Lord and is best for us and those for whom we pray.

In writing about the wisdom of God in fulfilling His promises in due season, Spurstowe also urges submissive praying. He says, "It is good in prayer to have the desires winged with affection and to be like an arrow drawn with full strength, but yet there must be a submission exercised unto the holy and wise will of God, that so it may appear that we seek him in a way of begging, and not by way of contest; that we make him not the object only of our duties and ourselves the end, but him to be both the object and the end of every service which we give unto him."[40] By submitting in prayer to God's wisdom and will, we show that what we want more than what we pray for is to glorify the Lord. We want His Name to be hallowed, and we trust Him to fulfill His promise to us when it best suits our welfare and His glory. We show that He is our portion, and there is nothing we desire besides Him (Ps. 73:25–26).

If the promises provide us a ground on which to pray, they also provide us a rule for how to pray. Leigh says we should pray for things as they are promised. Things absolutely promised should be absolutely asked for, with the great assurance that we will indeed, in the Lord's wise time and way, receive the thing He has pledged. But when the Lord has placed conditions and exceptions on a promise, our prayers must be conditional. We must then include some limitation on our prayers such as: "If God sees it to be good…"; "If it be according to His good pleasure…"; "If it may stand with His glory…"; or "If the Lord wills…."[41]

We should think back to the various kinds of promises outlined in chapter two. Once we see what kind of promise we are dealing with, we may pray in faith that God will do as He has spoken. If we are praying for spiritual things necessary to salvation, we may pray absolutely because the Lord has absolutely promised in Luke 11:13 that the Holy Spirit will be given to those who ask. If we are praying for help in temptation, we may absolutely pray for it because 1 Corinthians 10:13 absolutely

---

40. Spurstowe, 65.
41. Leigh, 41–42.

promises that with every temptation God will provide a way of escape so we may be able to endure it. Likewise, if we need wisdom to bear up under a trial, we may absolutely ask for it because James 1:5 says, "If any of you lack wisdom, let him ask of God, that giveth to all men liberally, and upbraideth not; and it shall be given him."

Even in such prayers for absolute promises, however, we must pray in submission to God's will and wisdom. Praying for things absolutely promised does not mean prescribing to God when or how He must keep His promise. We must trust Him with the circumstances of time, means, and measure, for He has reserved these things in His own power.[42] Spurstowe says, "God has in his Word recorded [the promises], as so many discoveries of his immutable counsel and purpose, that thereby faith might have a sure ground to rely upon him in all exigencies, and to expect a relief from him, but the season and time of performance, God has reserved to himself, as best knowing not only what to give, but when to give; so that, believers, though they may plead to God his promise, must yet be careful not to confine and limit him to times which they judge fittest; but wholly to resign themselves to his wise disposal, to whom every creature looks, and receive their meat in due season" (Ps. 145:15).[43] How important this reminder is for correcting our impatience!

If we pray for temporal things that are not absolutely promised to us, we must pray conditionally, asking for something insofar as it will glorify God and be for our spiritual good. We must also pray in the belief that God will give us either what we pray for or the equivalent. For example, if we pray for peace in a trial, we must trust that He will grant it if peace will glorify Him, but that if it will not, the Lord will give us patience in its place. For this blessing we have the Spirit to thank, who intercedes for us according to the will of God when we do not know what to pray for or when, in our ignorance or selfishness, we pray amiss. As Scripture promises, all things work together for our good as we are conformed to the image of Christ (Rom. 8:26–29). Take another example: If we pray for wealth or something as simple as a wage increase, we pray rightly when we believe that if it pleases God and will

---

42. Ibid., 43.
43. Spurstowe, 63–64.

be in our best interest, He will indeed increase our income. But we also pray that, believing that if it does not please God and would be a bane for our spirituality, He will supply us with the necessary contentment to make do with what we have.

Let us, then, strive to rightly use the promises of God, believing them, applying them, and praying them. This is the only way to profit from the instructions and doctrines set forth in the previous chapters. Knowledge is not meant to stay in our heads as abstract truth, but must be applied to real life so that we can enjoy its true blessings and real transformation. May the following chapters help you experience the inexhaustible richness and support of God's promises for all who call on Him in faith.

Study Questions

1. Why did the Puritans first instruct the mind about a given truth, then exhort the will so as to change the entire person? Why is their method of mind-will-action (or head-heart-hand) particularly useful in regard to God's promises?

2. Read Luke 24:25–26 and Hebrews 4:2. Why are we as believers slow to believe God's promises, even when we know they are true?

3. Why is faith in God's promises critical for our spiritual welfare? Describe the fruit of believing God's promises.

4. One of the devil's favorite tactics is to minimize the joys of the life of faith and to maximize the fleeting joys of this world. Explain how the devil is wrong by showing from the Scriptures and daily life how fruitful a life of faith in God's promises is and how barren a life of unbelief is.

5. Prove from Scripture the danger of embracing a mere assent-ing, historical faith. Why is it so important that faith penetrates our inmost soul?

6. How does William Spurstowe compare faith's view of God's promises to our view of the stars in the night sky? What lessons can we learn from this to strengthen our faith?

7. How can we in meditation "dive into the depths of the promise" and "make clefts into the promise," as Spurstowe advises?

8. Explain how God's promises are sufficient for any trials you may experience. How could you better keep God's promises on hand so that when doubts, sickness, and trials come, you are ready to meet them with the Word of God? Why should this encourage you to memorize God's promises?

9. How should we fight against impatience when the promises of God seem to offer no immediate relief?

10. Read Psalm 119:147. How does faith in God's promises help us pray to God? What does it mean to pray the promises? What does Leigh mean by saying, "To pray in faith is to go as far as the promise goes"?

Using God's Promises in Affliction

Everyone wants to avoid suffering. Suffering is painful, uncomfortable, humbling, and frustrating. Job 14:1 resonates with us when we suffer: "Man that is born of a woman is of few of days and full of trouble." Suffering is a part of life. Everywhere we turn, whether to newspapers or newscasts, we see that suffering is worldwide. No matter what the culture, the country, the class, or the age, people groan under some affliction.

Affliction may lead to despair, to chronic depression, or even to suicide. People who are afflicted think life is against them, that pain awaits them around every corner, and that suffering offers no way of escape. Some people turn to drugs and alcohol to escape suffering, but if these do not sufficiently numb their pain or misery, death may seem the only option. They reason that whatever is beyond the grave has to be better than the misery of this life.

As Christians, we have a better understanding of life—why it is so full of pain, why we must suffer, and why affliction and trial are universal. Scripture teaches us that our suffering is the consequence of the rebellion of our forebear, Adam, in the garden of Eden. Genesis 1:31 says that when "God saw everything that he had made…behold, it was very good." Neither suffering, nor pain, nor affliction, nor trial was a part of God's original creation, but as Ecclesiastes 7:29 says, "God hath made man upright; but they have sought out many inventions." The scheme that Adam sought in the garden of Eden was sinful and rebellious. God had forbidden Adam from eating fruit from the tree of the knowledge of good and evil, and had warned that disobedience would result in death (Gen. 2:17). But Adam ate from the tree anyway. Since he was the representative of the entire human race, his rebellion plunged us all into sin and placed us under the penalty of death (Rom. 5:12, 19a; Eph. 2:1–3).

The life of suffering and death that we face as humans is not the life that God gave us at creation, but one that resulted from our disobedience. Indeed, we suffer in daily installments the wages of our rebellion against God (Rom. 6:23a). While faith in Christ does not make us immune from this lot of humanity, it changes the tenor of it, because the One who sovereignly apportions the trials is no longer an angry Judge but our heavenly Father.

This means we can face trials in the strength of Christ and we can find blessings in trials through the work of Christ. We are blessed because of the faithful application of the promises of God to our various trials (1 Peter 1:6), and because our certain and abiding hope in the midst of suffering rests in what God has promised us *in* our trials and *by* our trials. In our trials, God promises us His presence and protection; by our trials, He promises us correction and spiritual benefits. Let us examine these promises in more depth after first considering how faith in Christ changes the tenor of our afflictions.

Why Afflictions Are Necessary

Scripture teaches us that afflictions and trials are a necessary part of the Christian pilgrimage. In his letter to the Philippians, Paul encourages believers to stand firm for the Lord, reminding them, "For unto you it is given in the behalf of Christ, not only to believe on him, but also to suffer for his sake" (1:29). He connects belief in Christ with suffering for Christ, seeing them both as gifts granted to the church. In the epistle to the Romans, Paul says we are adopted as children of God, making us coheirs with Christ, but our inheritance in glory is conditional on our suffering with Christ in this life. He writes, "The Spirit itself beareth witness with our spirit, that we are the children of God: and if children, then heirs; heirs of God and joint-heirs with Christ; if so be that we suffer with him, that we may be also glorified together" (8:16–17).

When Paul and Barnabas took the gospel to Lystra (Acts 14:8–18), Jews from Antioch and Iconium persuaded a crowd of people to stone Paul. Knowing that suffering was part of his calling as an apostle (cf. Acts 9:15–16) and of his pilgrimage, Paul returned to Lystra, "confirming the souls of the disciples, and exhorting them to continue in the faith, and that we must through much tribulation enter into the kingdom of God" (14:22). Peter wrote his first epistle to the "strangers scattered throughout…" (1 Peter 1:1), who were suffering for their faith in Christ. He encouraged them to stand fast and trust the Lord, fixing their hope on His promise of deliverance upon Christ's return (1:7). But Peter goes on to say: "Beloved, think it not strange concerning the fiery trial which is to try you, as though some strange thing happened unto you: But rejoice, inasmuch as ye are partakers of Christ's sufferings; that, when his glory shall be revealed, ye may be glad also with exceeding joy" (4:12–13).

Suffering is to be expected, not only as part of our human experience, but also as part of our Christian pilgrimage heavenward. Our suffering, whether a direct result of our faith and defense of the cause of Christ, or something we bear as part of the fallen world, should not surprise us. However, because we are Christians, and therefore heirs of the promises of God, our trials and afflictions have a different purpose—they sanctify us within the grand scheme of God's redemption of our souls.

Afflictions are the instruments by which God, as Master Carpenter, shapes and conforms us to Christ's image (Rom. 8:28–29). They are the means by which God completes the good work He began in us (Phil. 1:6–7). They are occasions for our faith to grow in steadfastness and maturity (James 1:2–4). They are the means by which God exposes our sin to lead us to repentance (Job 42:3b, 5–6) and to reveal our hearts (Gen. 22:1, 12). And they are necessary goads sent to test the genuineness of our faith and prepare us for the return of Christ (1 Peter 1:6–7; Matt. 10:22b).

It is thus foolish for us to think we can avoid trials, difficulties, and affliction as Christians. Why would we want to? If they serve such an important purpose within God's plan of redemption, we cannot afford to live without them. Indeed, we should prefer to live with them. That is what the apostle concluded when he realized how much his trials had benefited him. He says: "Most gladly therefore will I rather glory in my infirmities, that the power of Christ may rest upon me. Therefore I take pleasure in infirmities, in reproaches, in necessities, in persecutions, in distresses for Christ's sake: for when I am weak, then am I strong" (2 Cor. 12:9b–10).

With such hope before us, let us look further at what God promises us in our afflictions, for without His presence and protection, they might break us.

God's Promise of Protection from Afflictions

While God offers us many promises *in* our afflictions, we should note that He also promises to keep us *from* afflictions and dangers. Let us consider first that God promises, in keeping with His glory and our eternal good, that He will protect us from trials and afflictions that might undo us. Indeed, we pray in the Lord's Prayer that God will "deliver us from evil" (Matt. 6:13). But if the Lord, in His wisdom and goodness, has determined that He will be most glorified and we best served by an affliction, we should consider the many promises God offers to saints in the midst of their trials.

God often promises that He will preserve us from trial. The LORD promised Abram, "Fear not, Abram, I am thy shield" (Gen. 15:1). Likewise, Agur says, "Every word of God is pure: he is a shield unto them that put their trust in him" (Prov. 30:5). But note that we find refuge *behind* a shield. Rather than being something material or tangible, this protection is the "word of God." How can a word serve as a shield? This word does not refer to the commands of Scripture, which we are to obey. Neither does this word refer to threats of Scripture, which restrain our disobedience and breed holy fear. *Word*, then, must refer to God's promises, for these alone tell us what God will do to comfort us.[1] We find protection against affliction and preservation from trial and dan-

---

1. Leigh, 7. See also chapter 1: a promise is a declaration of God's will concerning good to be received by us or evil which He will remove from us.

ger by hiding behind the refuge of God's promises. Just as the shield of faith extinguishes the fiery darts of the enemy (Eph. 6:16), so God's promises to prevent afflictions are a shield of protection.

In the book of Jeremiah, the Lord described the prophet's ministry, promising to protect him and preserve him from the harm conceived in the evil hearts of the people of Judah. God said: "For, behold, I have made thee this day a defenced city, and an iron pillar, and brazen walls against the whole land, against the kings of Judah, against the princes thereof, against the priests thereof, and against the people of the land. And they shall fight against thee; but they shall not prevail against thee; for I am with thee, said the LORD, to deliver thee." (1:18–19). The bronze wall that surrounded Jeremiah was the Lord Himself. Surely Jeremiah was comforted by this promise as he prophesied to wicked people who threatened him.

God uses other images to assure us of His protection in the midst of trial. In Zechariah 2:5, the Lord says He will be "a wall of fire round about" His people. Psalm 125:2 proclaims, "As the mountains are round about Jerusalem, so the LORD is round about his people." Psalm 121:7 states, "The LORD shall preserve thee from all evil: he shall preserve thy soul." Psalm 91:9–11 says the Lord encompasses us, protects us from all evil, and sends His angels to watch over us in all our ways. The psalm assures us: "Because thou hast made the LORD, which is my refuge, even the most High, thy habitation; there shall no evil befall thee, neither shall any plague come nigh thy dwelling. For he shall give his angels charge over thee, to keep thee in all thy ways." And in Job 5:19, Eliphaz assures us of God's protection when he says, "He shall deliver thee in six troubles: yea, in seven there shall no evil touch thee."

These promises are shields against trial and preservation in the midst of affliction and danger. Let these promises comfort and assure you that whatever trial you face, the Lord is your shield. As Edward Leigh says, "Therefore such who are in covenant with God may look to be freed from evils and dangers, if it be for their good."[2]

---

2. Ibid., 116.

Though God protects us from many trials, He permits others to strike us. When affliction does strike, we know that God in His infinite wisdom and boundless goodness has determined that this trial will bring Him the most glory and us eternal good. This alone helps us face affliction with contentment, trust, and patience. But the Lord also promises us two things in the midst of trial: His comforting and sustaining presence, and His protection against our ruin.

God's Promise of His Presence in Our Afflictions

The account in Daniel 3 of three young men who were thrown into a fiery furnace is memorable for its record of holy resolve, trust, loyalty, and faith. But it also shows us God's presence with His people in affliction. When King Nebuchadnezzar threw Shadrach, Meshach, and Abednego into a furnace that was so hot that the men who threw them in were "burned alive," the Lord Himself was with the young believers. The king asked: "Did not we cast three men bound into the midst of the fire? Lo I see four men loose, walking in the midst of the fire, and they have no hurt" (Dan. 3:24–25). Leigh comments, "God will be with his [people] in the fire, as he was with the three children; and in the water, as he was with Moses and Jonah."[3] God's presence changes everything.

Likewise, Jesus was with His disciples in a boat when a storm arose on the Lake of Galilee (Mark 4:35–41). The storm was so ferocious that the disciples feared for their lives. They had forgotten who was with them in the boat. It was Christ, who not only had created the sea but now governed it. God revealed Himself to Job as the One "who shut up the sea with doors...and brake up for it my decreed place, and set bars and doors, and said, Hitherto shalt thou come, and no further, and here shall thy proud waves be stayed" (Job 38:8–11). Jesus demonstrated this protection when He commanded the storm and waves to be still, and they obeyed. His presence with His disciples made the difference. No wonder Jesus asked: "Why are ye so fearful? how is it that ye have no

---

3. Ibid.

faith?" (Mark 4:40). The disciples had no cause to fear, for Christ was with them.

Many Christians have found comfort in Isaiah 43:1–3, in which God assures us: "Fear not: for I have redeemed thee; I have called thee by thy name, thou art mine. When thou passest through the waters, I will be with thee; and through the rivers, they shall not overflow thee; when thou walkest through the fire thou shalt not be burned; neither shall the flame kindle upon thee. For I am the LORD thy God, the Holy One of Israel, thy Savior." Israel had no reason to fear affliction because God was with them. Likewise, the Lord was with Israel in Babylon. He told Ezekiel, "Although I have cast them far off among the heathen, and although I have scattered them among the countries, yet will I be to them as a little sanctuary" (Ezek. 11:16).

The Psalms also assure us of the Lord's comfort in affliction. In Psalm 23:4, David says, "Yea, though I walk through the valley of the shadow of death, I will fear no evil." What gave David such strength in the face of danger and death and helped him overcome fear was the Lord. As David says, "For thou art with me; thy rod and thy staff they comfort me." In Psalm 91:15, the Lord also assures us of His presence in the midst of danger. He says, "He shall call upon me, and I will answer him: I will be with him in trouble."

These verses acknowledge that though we are not exempt from trials, we may enjoy incomparable blessing in them, namely, the presence of the Lord. Leigh says, "In the valley of the shadow of death, [the saints] may assure themselves of God's merciful, omnipotent presence."[4] Having that, we have all.

God's Promise of Protection Against Ruin

Besides being with us in our trials, God also promises to protect us from being ruined by them. Of Isaiah 43:2, Leigh says: "Fire and water are two merciless enemies, yet the fire shall not burn, nor the waters overflow them, as God has promised.... They must not pass by these,

---

4. Ibid.

by the fire and by the water, but *through the fire, and through the water.*"[5] While God keeps us from some trials, He may deem it better for us to face others. Leigh says we must not *pass* by those trials but go *through* them. At times, afflictions seem bigger than life, but the Lord promises to preserve us in them from ultimate ruin.

Job is the best example of such suffering. He endured incredible pain and loss. He lost his possessions, his children, the support of his wife and his friends, and his health. But as we learn from the first two chapters of Job, his afflictions were ordained by God, not to destroy him or punish him for his sin, but to test him (cf. Gen. 22:1), so that God might reveal more of Himself to Job and more of Job to himself (Job 42:1–6). Though this text does not reveal a direct promise to Job for his encouragement, we find much for our encouragement. In the first chapters of this book we catch a glimpse into God's mind and intent regarding Job's trials (and thus ours as well), as well as the care and protection of God in His covenant relationship with Job, which governs His decisions about which trials to permit and which to prevent.

The Lord's intent in Job's trials can also be seen in their outcome (Job 42:3–6), when Job says, "Therefore have I uttered that I understood not; things too wonderful for me, which I knew not…I have heard of thee by the hearing of the ear, but now mine eye seeth thee; wherefore I abhor myself, and repent in dust and ashes." These verses reveal the Lord's purposes for Job's trials, which were for Job's good. Though Job's pain and losses were not minimized one whit, he learned that God was protecting him from ultimate ruin, and, in time, would double all the blessings he had lost (cf. Job 1:3; 42:10, 12).

This behind-the-scenes look also teaches us that God's covenant relationship with us eternally secures our Father's care and protection. In God's providence, He allows us to suffer only trials that work for our good. He prevents us from enduring trials that would destroy us.

We thus may be comforted that when afflictions come, the Lord Himself will be with us. He will pass through the fire with us. He will never leave us or forsake us. Like the log that Moses threw into the

---

5. Ibid.

bitter waters at Marah to make them sweet, God promises us His sweetening presence in every affliction. When afflictions strike and terrors encompass us, we have the abiding hope that God will uphold us and fulfill His good purposes for us, for His steadfast love is great to the heavens and His faithfulness to the clouds (Ps. 57:2, 4, 10).

God's Promise of Wise and Tender Correction

The Lord also promises to *use* our afflictions for our eternal good. This is because we undergo trials not as enemies of God, but as children of God through our saving relationship with Christ. To those without Christ, trials are but foretastes of the coming judgment, but to we who are in Christ, trials are mediated by God's eternal grace and love. The Lord has promised our correction and spiritual benefit through our afflictions. Keeping this in mind will help us face our troubles with the view of how we can profit from them rather than how long we have to suffer.

Because we, like sheep, tend to stray from the path of following God, one of the primary purposes of affliction is to restore us to the path or hedge in the path so that we do not leave it. Hebrews 12:6 says, "For whom the Lord loveth he chasteneth, and scourgeth every son whom he receiveth." That by itself is a comfort because, as the passage goes on to say, "But if ye be without chastisement, whereof all are partakers, then are ye bastards, and not sons" (v. 8). As Leigh puts it, "He that escapes his affliction, may suspect his adoption."[6] So we have comfort in affliction that our Father is reproving us because He loves us and is correcting us because we are His. Even more, His correction is done in great wisdom and with much tenderness.

As parents, we correct our children as seems best to us (Heb. 12:10) to bring them to obedience, but our wise Father considers what is the best means of our correction, what is most just, and what is the necessary duration, not so much to bring about our obedience as that we may share His holiness and enjoy the peaceful fruit of righteousness (Heb. 12:10–11). In Jeremiah 46:28, the Lord tells His people that their afflic-

---

6. Ibid., 119.

tion will not destroy them, "but correct thee in measure." That is, it will be catered in divine wisdom and love to their spiritual need. What Paul says of temptation in 1 Corinthians 10:13 could also be said of affliction: "God is faithful, who will not suffer you to be tempted above that ye are able; but will with the temptation also make a way to escape, that ye may be able to bear it." Thus, we should take comfort in the midst of trial that our all-wise God knows what is best for us.

Similarly, when the Lord corrects us by affliction, He promises to temper it with great compassion and tenderness (Lam. 3:31–32). He does not execute His burning anger on us (Hos. 11:9), but acts as a compassionate father who is aware of our frailty. Psalm 103:13–14 says: "Like as a father pitieth his children, so the Lord pitieth them that fear him. For he knoweth our frame; he remembereth that we are dust." Hosea 2:14–15 says the Lord will speak tenderly to us in our afflictions: "Therefore, behold, I will allure her, and bring her into the wilderness, and speak comfortably to her. And I will give her her vineyards from thence, and the Valley of Achor for a door of hope." When the Lord must correct our sin, He is impatient over our misery (Judg. 10:16) and does not keep His anger forever (Jer. 3:12) because He delights in steadfast love (Mic. 7:18).

God's Promise to Mature Us in Faith

Romans 8:28 says, "And we know that all things work together for good to them that love God, to them who are the called according to his purpose." This verse brings us great comfort since "all things" refers to trials and afflictions. Paul speaks of the "sufferings of this present time" (v. 18), which cause us to "groan within ourselves, waiting for the adoption, to wit, the redemption of our body" (v. 23). Yet in the midst of this suffering and groaning, we have the assurance that "the Spirit helps us in our weakness" and "intercedes for [us] according to the will of God" (vv. 26, 27). Because our suffering is for our glorification (vv. 17–18), and the Spirit intercedes for us to ensure that outcome (vv. 26–27), we *know* that all things work together for good for those who love God and are called according to His purpose as His children whom He has made coheirs with Christ (vv. 16–17). God promises that our afflictions are remedial and sanctifying. He puts us through trials to bring blessing to us and to reveal what is in us, which serve to purge us of sin and to quicken our graces.

First, God promises to bless us in afflictions. Romans 8:28–29 says our present sufferings conform us to the image of Christ. James 1:2–4 tells us to rejoice when we go through trials since the testing of our faith produces endurance, which leads to maturity. Matthew 5:10–12 and 1 Peter 3:14 say we will be blessed if we suffer for righteousness' sake. And Romans 5:3–5 says, "And not only so, but we glory in tribulations also: knowing that tribulation worketh patience; and patience, experience; and experience, hope: and hope maketh not ashamed; because the love of God is shed abroad in our hearts by the Holy Ghost which is given unto us." Paul adds in 2 Corinthians 4:16–17: "For which cause we faint not; but though our outward man perish, yet the inward man is renewed day by day. For our light affliction, which is but for a moment, worketh for us a far more exceeding and eternal weight of glory." Leigh comments, "We shall have for affliction, glory; for light affliction, heavy, massy substantial glory, a weight of glory; for momentary affliction, eternal glory."[7]

Second, God promises that our afflictions test us and reveal what is in us. The Lord does this, not to learn something He does not know about us, but that we might be confronted with either a strength of which we were unaware (which He placed in us) or with a weakness of which we were unaware or unwilling to address (so that we might be brought to repentance). Like the stick Elisha threw into the water to make an ax head float (2 Kings 6:5–7), trial has a way of causing what is in us to surface.

The Lord brought unimaginable affliction on Abraham when He commanded him to sacrifice his only son (Gen. 22), through whom God had promised the messianic Seed would come as a blessing to the nations (Gen. 21:12). Such a trial would reveal whether Abraham loved his son more than God; whether he believed God would keep His prom-

---

7. Ibid.

ise concerning His son, even when this present command appeared to contradict it; and whether he trusted God's ways even though he did not understand them. Abraham did love God more than Isaac; he believed God; and he trusted God's ways. Hebrews 11 says, "By faith Abraham, when he was tried, offered up Isaac...accounting that God was able to raise him up, even from the dead" (vv. 17, 19). The trial revealed what would prove to be a strength to Abraham and to all the saints to follow. Through this trial, Abraham's faith endured and matured (James 1:2–4), making him the father of the faithful (Rom. 4:11) and the friend of God (James 2:23).

When Moses led the people of Israel out of Egypt, they soon came to what seemed like a dead end: the Red Sea (Ex. 14). God told them to set up camp facing the sea. In the meantime, Pharaoh and his army were in feverish pursuit of the Israelites. The Israelites saw the army approaching and were "sore afraid," saying to Moses, "Because there were no graves in Egypt, hast thou taken us away to die in the wilderness? wherefore hast thou dealt thus with us, to carry us forth out of Egypt? Is not this the word that we did tell thee in Egypt, saying, Let us alone, that we may serve the Egyptians?" (vv. 10–12).

When the twelve spies were sent into Canaan to spy out the land that God had promised to give to Israel, only two spies believed that God could lead them in victory against the inhabitants and help them posses the land. Caleb said, "Let us go up at once, and possess it; for we are well able to overcome it" (Num. 13:30). The other ten spies brought back a bad report, saying, "We be not able to go up against the people, for they are stronger than we" (v. 31). When Israel heard these two conflicting reports, they were terrified and said to Moses, "Would God that we had died in the land of Egypt! Or would God we had died in this wilderness! And wherefore hath the LORD brought us unto this land, to fall by the sword?" (14:2b–3a).

Both the confrontation at the Red Sea and the confrontation at the border of Canaan were tests God used to try His people's hearts. Would they trust Him, follow Him into battle, and obey Him against all odds? In short, did they believe Him? The response to both tests was unbelief. His people did not believe Him. His people would not obey Him. God's people did not trust Him. Of such examples the apostle Paul writes, "Now these things took place as examples for us, that we might not lust after evil things as they did" (1 Cor. 10:6). But the apostle goes on to say, "Now all these things happened unto them for examples: and they are written for our admonition…. Wherefore let him that thinketh he standeth take heed lest he fall" (vv. 11–12).

The point is that afflictions and suffering may be the human lot, but we do not endure them as unbelievers do, for we have the promise of God that all things, especially afflictions, work together for our good. They work for good because God, in His goodness and love to us for Christ's sake, sanctifies them to us on our journey heavenward. God uses our afflictions to correct and discipline us, though He does so with much compassion and tenderness. He uses our afflictions to test us so that weakness or grace may surface. When grace is quickened by trial, we move forward with greater confidence and stand as an encouragement to others of God's faithfulness to grow His people in holiness. Likewise, when weakness is quickened by trial, we may repent of it, stay closer to Christ in our walk, better guard our hearts, and press on in our labors with greater caution and humility. May God help us know the great comfort of His promises in our afflictions so that we can rejoice in our sufferings and face our trials with holy patience. For He has promised us that, "But the God of all grace, who hath called us unto his eternal glory by Christ Jesus, after that ye have suffered a while, make you perfect, stablish, strengthen, settle you" (1 Peter 5:10).

Steps to Take in Times of Affliction

The Puritans provide us with a variety of ways or steps to take in times of affliction. Here is a summary of them:

1. Choose some verses that speak of God's assurance of His presence and protection in trials and meditate upon them so that you will not be at a loss for support and comfort when hard times come. In this way, you will prepare your heart for trials and will not be surprised when they come.

2. Consider what William Spurstowe says of the blessed promise of the Lord's presence and protection in Isaiah 43:2: "To them who are full of fears through the approach of dangers, which they have no hope to avoid, or power to overcome, how full of encouragement and comfort is that promise of *protection* and safety."[8] Meditate on this promise, for it will greatly help you and prepare you to meet afflictions, assuring you of God's presence and your protection.

3. See the great dangers that Isaiah 43 says we will encounter. Are there any greater dangers than fire or flood? With the help of a friend, you may survive a battle, outlive a prison sentence, or bear the curse of exile, but what can a friend do for you in fire or flood but perish alongside you? The Lord says that in fire or flood He will be with you. As Spurstowe says, "In the swelling waters and in the devouring flames none can be a relief to any but God; and he has promised to believers to be with them in the midst of both of these, [so that] in the greatest extremities which can befall them they may fully rest assured, that nothing can separate God from them, but that he will either give them deliverance from troubles, or support them under troubles."[9] What sweet nectar do such promises deliver to your heart?

4. Do not just assent to the promises; take them in hand as you would a staff and lean on them. Gray says: "As you would not destroy your own souls, be much in making use and application of the promises. Are not the promises your life? Did not all the saints that went to heaven before us, go to heaven living upon the promises? There was not a step of Abraham's life, but he walked with a promise in it; there was not an affliction that Abraham met with, but he took comfort to himself from the promises."[10]

5. Comfort yourself with these words: "God assures me, he will lay no more on me, than I shall be able to bear, either my burden shall be made lighter or my faith stronger."[11]

6. Remember that God promises not only to uphold and sustain you in afflictions (Pss. 9:9; 37:4, 39–40), but also that His abundant con-

8. Spurstowe, 94.
9. Ibid., 94–95.
10. Gray, 138.
11. Leigh, 125.

solations and comfort will break forth upon your afflictions and shatter your troubles as light that breaks forth in the morning and shatters the darkness that so long lies upon the night (Ps. 112:4; Mic. 7:8–9; 2 Cor. 1:5).[12]

7. Take comfort that your trials are a sign, not of God's abandonment or anger, but of your sonship and Christian pedigree (Heb. 12:5–7). View your sufferings as proof of your identity in Christ and of God's commitment to you as your heavenly Father.

8. In all your afflictions, trust God. Faith sees life in death, assurance of deliverance in the deepest distress. Faith teaches you to say, "God has chastised me according to His threats, therefore He will comfort me according to His promises" (see Jer. 32:42). As Leigh says: "Has not God promised and assured me not to fail nor forsake me, but to uphold me in affliction and bring me through it and comfort me by it and glorify me after it? Then I should with Abraham hope against hope, and apprehend the certain accomplishment of these promises by faith when sense and carnal reason sees nothing but the contrary."[13]

9. As you will be saved by faith after death, so you must live by faith in this world. If you rely on God's mercy for your soul, you must depend on His providence for your body. How does he trust God for a kingdom who will not trust Him for a crust of bread?[14]

10. You must believe the promises and not merely assent to them. They will be as a meadow of flowers to you and you as a lazy bee to them if you do not really believe in them and apply them. Just as the industry of the bee extracts the honey, so the industry of your faith extracts comfort from God's promises.[15] Did not David find it to be so in Psalm 119:49–50?

11. A lively and vital faith in the promises of God helps you exercise patience in afflictions. As Andrew Gray writes: "If you would inquire of faith in the midnight of your affliction, what is its opinion of God

---

12. Ibid., 122.
13. Ibid., 128.
14. Ibid., 138.
15. Spurstowe, 278.

and of your own estate, it would sweetly answer you thus: 'Wait upon God for I shall yet praise Him. If it seems slow, wait for it; comfort and relief will surely come; it will not delay.' For faith does not entertain ill thoughts of God and is therefore the noble interpreter of a Christian's afflictions." Gray continues: "If you likewise were to inquire of sense, reason, and unbelief what is their interpretation of your affliction, they would have you cry unto God: 'Why have you become to me as an enemy or a liar?' But if you heed faith's interpretation, it will have you cry out, 'I know the thoughts of His heart, that they are thoughts of peace and not of evil, to bring me to a good and blessed end. Now I sow in tears, but then I shall reap in joy. Now I weep, but joy comes in the morning.'"[16]

12. The purpose of chastisement is often to amend our ways, which is why it is called "correction," which means to set right or straight. Therefore, when a trial comes, you must try to uncover the sin for which God is correcting you (Job 36:9). When you have found it, be humbled by it, make your peace with God, and reform yourself (John 5:14). Then you may expect God's sweet comfort, for the comfort of a sinner reformed by corrections is as plentiful and excellent as the brightness of the noonday sun, and as constant and durable as the light of the morning (Job 11:14–18).[17]

13. Do not despise your afflictions, but see them as necessary trials that help you to better know God and yourself (Prov. 17:3; Zech. 13:9). As the skill of a pilot is unknown except in a tempest, and the valor of a captain is unseen but in a battle, so the worth of a Christian is untried except in a trial and temptation. If afflictions are sovereign medicines to kill spiritual diseases, look to the Lord to purge your sin, to refine you as silver in a crucible, and comfort yourself that you will lose nothing but the dross (Isa. 1:25–26).[18]

14. Examine your heart and life for harbored sin, for unrepented iniquity. This, of course, is not the reason behind every trial, but more often than not, our continuance in sin and impenitence are the

---

16. Gray, 161.
17. Leigh, 125–26.
18. Ibid., 120.

occasion for God's Fatherly chastisement of us (Ps. 32:1–4; Heb. 12:4–14).

15. The covenant of grace is the measure of God's obligation to us, and the covenant includes chastisement, when necessary, as part of God's expression of loving care toward us and His self-binding to sanctify us in holiness. God has "kept to himself this prerogative of chastening the delinquencies of his children with rods [Ps. 89:30–35], of withdrawing his favors from them, when they withhold their obedience to him; of exercising the severity of a Father, as well as the indulgency of a Mother."[19]

16. When you lack the staff of outward comforts in your hand and feel the pain of the rod of affliction on your back, "do not suspect God's fidelity in his promises, but reflect upon [your]self, and by a serious disquisition to consider from whence the suspension of any good things that he has promised, arises."[20]

17. Go to the Lord in your affliction and say: "Lord, it is part of thy covenant to deliver me from such a cross and calamity; Lord, thou hast said that the rod of the wicked shall not rest upon the lot of the righteous; that thou wilt afflict, but in measure, according to our strength, and for our good. O sanctify thy hand unto me, give me faith and patience to wait upon thee, wisdom to make a good use of this chastisement; let it purge me from my dross, and breed the quiet fruit of righteousness."[21]

18. Let your afflictions drive you to greater fellowship and communion with God. Let affliction make you seek out God's promise, and let the promise stir up your faith. So let your faith lead you to prayer, for in your prayer you will find God (Jer. 29:10–14; Mic. 7:7). Who would not be content with a wet spring if it guaranteed a bountiful harvest? So be content for afflictions to rest upon you, for you have this promise, that they will procure and further your chief good— the welfare and happiness of your eternal soul.[22]

---

19. Spurstowe, 230–31.
20. Ibid., 231.
21. Leigh, 125.
22. Ibid., 121, 124.

19. In all the perils of this life, whether sickness, war, famine, thieves, or any trial whatsoever, call to mind the promises and quiet your soul with this assurance: that none of these afflictions shall steal away your amenities or shorten your days more than shall turn out to both your present and eternal good (Mark 10:28–30).[23]

20. Plead in your prayers the hopes that God's promises offer you in affliction, asking not when you will be delivered from the trial, but what the trial is meant to deliver unto you. Since the Lord has sent it for your good, pray for it to be sanctified unto you, to work a healing in you, to be remedial in its effect, and to be a cause of rejoicing both in the midst of it and when you come to the other side of it.

21. Remind yourself that the exaltation, glory, and crown that Christ now enjoys were preceded by His sufferings, and if we would follow Him we must walk the same path (Matt. 10:24–25).

22. When afflictions eat away at your worldly comforts and enjoyments, whether possessions, health, work, finances, friends, freedom, or whatever else might be as easily lost as gained, remind yourself of your chief end: to glorify God and enjoy Him forever. All temporal things that you enjoy in life are, by God's saving grace, made subservient to this chief end. Whatever temporal comforts and enjoyments are conducive to that end, God promises to give in abundance. But whatever temporal amenities would be harmful to you and hinder you from your end, God mercifully and graciously promises to take away.[24] Do you not do the same for your children, taking from them or keeping from them those things, though they desire them with all their hearts, that you know by experience or understanding will actually hurt or hinder them in their course? God is doing the same for you, though with infinite wisdom and a bottomless ocean of love.

23. You must believe also that whatever you lose in this life, your Father is trading for that which is infinitely and eternally better. The promises have their certainty of fulfillment in God's faithfulness in that He cannot lie, but they have their manner of fulfillment in God's wisdom in that He knows what is best. So in temporal promises, God will either give the thing promised or that which is its better equiva-

---

23. Ibid., 142.
24. Spurstowe, 227.

lent. If you pray for health, God will either give it or the strength to endure sickness, whichever is better. Likewise, if you pray for deliverance, He will either give deliverance or comfort in trial, whichever is better. Thus, God does not break His promise, but changes it to the better, catering His fulfillments to whatever will most benefit you spiritually and support your chief end. You may have to undergo the darkness of the grave, but He will preserve you from its corruption (Ps. 16:10).[25]

24. Remember in the midst of your most grievous afflictions that the worst state of a believer is better than the best state of an unbeliever. Though your supplications and tears are to no avail here, yet in heaven your prayers are registered and your tears bottled. Your sanctified afflictions are better than the unbeliever's unsanctified enjoyments. Their morsels are rolled up in the filth of their sin and in the bitterness of God's curses, while all your emptiness and lack are both sweetened and supplied by God's promises. They have good things in this life while you have yours reserved for the other. You may have a hungry body but they have starved souls. Though your body is a parched wilderness, your soul is a well-watered garden (John 7:38). They measure their happiness by a false rule and their height by their shadows. Ahab may have ridden in the chariot, but Elijah ran before it. They are the favorites of earth but the enemies of heaven; you are the enemy of earth but the favorite of heaven.[26]

25. Learn to judge happiness not by the light of sense but by the lamp of the sanctuary, and in time you will see that nothing can be a foundation of happiness to you that does not have its stability from the promise of God.[27]

25. Ibid., 228–30.
26. Ibid., 255–65.
27. Ibid., 265.

Study Questions

1. Show from Scripture why afflictions are necessary for believers. Why should we be less surprised when we suffer than when we do not?

2. List ten benefits from your afflictions that God graciously works out within you. Supply scriptural proof.

3. What pictures does God use to assure us of His protection in the midst of trial?

4. Sometimes a married couple dreads to go separate ways for even a few days. When they reunite, they lovingly tell each other, "Your presence changes everything for me." How does God's presence change everything for a believer? Why should the promise of God's presence in our afflictions mean more than life to us?

5. How do God's promises of support in our affliction work for our eternal good?

6. If afflictions do the believer so much good, should we encourage believers to pray for more affliction? Why or why not? (Read Matthew 6:34)

7. God promises to correct His people only in measure, and with each trial He will provide a way of escape so that they may be able to bear it (1 Cor. 10:13). Why do we have so much trouble trusting that God knows what is best for us? Why are we prone to distrust the Lord when He has such a good track record with us?

8. Read Matthew 15:21–28. How did God use trials to mature the Canaanite woman's faith? Explain a few ways in which God has used afflictions to mature you in faith.

9. Which one of the twenty-five steps to take in time of affliction helped you the most? Which do you need to work on the most?

10. Read Hebrews 12:10–11. How does sanctified affliction make us partakers of Christ's righteousness and holiness? In what other ways should we consider Christ in times of personal affliction?

Using God's Promises in Times of Temptation and Sin

God rescues us as believers from the kingdom of darkness and brings us into the kingdom of light. Colossians 1:13–14 says: "[God] hath delivered us from the power of darkness, and hath translated us into the kingdom of his dear Son: in whom we have redemption through his blood, even the forgiveness of sins."

The joy this deliverance brings to us is indescribable. Words fail to express it; it fills our hearts to overflowing. Once we were blind, but now we see; once we were deaf, but now we hear; once we were dead, but now we live. The praises of God are on our lips, the peace of forgiveness fills our hearts, the lordship of Christ governs our affections, grace streams through our eyes and ears, and the blessings that await us in heaven transform our minds.

Meantime, Satan fumes with rage at having lost his citizens. Like Pharaoh of Egypt, he will not sit idly by and watch his slaves walk away from his dominion. He therefore sets out with his vast and dark army in hot pursuit of us (Ex. 14:5–8).

Knowing he cannot challenge the King of kings, Satan challenges the host of Christ's redeemed. Since it is impossible to reclaim us (due to the keeping power of our new Lord of lords), he tries to provoke Him to cast us off. He tirelessly tempts us to sin, setting traps for our feet, lures for our hearts, sirens for our ears, and enticements for our eyes in the hope that, when we sin, God will cast us off as worthless rogues, unworthy of His love, mercy, grace, and promises.

It is clear, then, that our redemption in Christ from Satan's dominion is the reason for our temptations. While we were under Satan's tyranny, sin was as natural to us as the air we breathe and as comfortable to us as the bed in which we sleep (Eph. 4:17–19). Blind and deaf to the truth in Jesus (Eph. 4:21), we were ignorant of our bondage to sin and our accursed state. But now that Christ has delivered us from sin, we have joined the church militant, over which Christ is Lord, and have become targets of Satan's malice and rage (1 Peter 5:8–9). As long as we were asleep in his dungeon, Satan cared nothing about us—what we did, what we thought, what we said, what we felt, and what motivated us to action. But now that the Spirit of God dwells in us (Rom. 8:9) and we are new creatures in Christ (2 Cor. 5:17), set free from the slavery of sin (John 8:34, 36), Satan opposes us at every turn, tempting us to sin against Christ and trying at all costs to slip us out of the safety of His hands (John 10:28–29).

So our struggle against sin will continue until Christ returns and at last redeems us from Satan. Paul was longing for that final release when he cried out: "O wretched man that I am! who shall deliver me from the body of this death?" (Rom. 7:24). This hope so enraptured him that he taunted death and the grave, saying: "O death, where is thy sting? O grave, where is thy victory?... Thanks be to God, which giveth us the victory through our Lord Jesus Christ" (1 Cor. 15:55, 57).

Are we thus without hope today? Have we no relief in our present struggles against temptation? Though Satan cannot have us at the last, are we doomed to be sifted as wheat (Luke 22:31–32) until Christ delivers us? Given our great weakness, what if we slide back into prolonged and gross sin? Is there no hope for us until the end? If, perchance, we do come to ourselves, as the Prodigal Son did (Luke 15:17–19), will our heavenly Father receive us again? Will He heal us of our backslidings? These questions plague many of God's people and steal much of their joy.

Our only hope is to trust the promises of God in times of temptation and sin. But before we can draw comfort and hope from the promises that relate to temptation, we must first understand three things about temptation.

We Are Not Alone in Temptation[1]

Some of the most common, but no less erroneous, conceptions among Christians include: "I'm the only one struggling with this sin," "No one struggles as much as I do," or "Everyone has overcome their sins but me." It is hard not to think these thoughts when victory over a particular sin seems elusive or when we get blindsided by temptations over which we thought we had victory. But, truly, the common condition of all the godly is to be tempted.[2] Paul makes this point in 1 Corinthians 10:13 when he says, "There hath no temptation taken you but such as is common to man."

One person will struggle more with lust than another or more with anger than another, but temptation is universal among God's people. Do you struggle with lust? David succumbed to adultery. Do you struggle with anger? David was an accomplice to murder. Do you struggle with fear? Peter denied the Lord and Abraham lied to Abimelech about his wife. From the most mature Christian to the one with the tiniest seed of faith, all of God's people suffer temptations and battle against the adversary, Satan.

Having been joined to God as His children by grace, we are also His soldiers (Eph. 6:10–18). Satan is now as much our enemy as he is Christ's. Having tempted Christ (Matt. 4:1–10), the devil now tempts us (Luke 22:31); having tempted the parents (Gen. 3:1; Rev. 12:13), he will tempt their children (1 Peter 5:8; Rev. 12:17). If it were not so, the apostle would not have told us to "walk circumspectly" (Eph. 5:15), to "be strong in the Lord, and in the power of his might" (Eph. 6:10), or to "put on the whole armor of God, that ye may be able to stand against the wiles of the devil" (Eph. 6:11). Such warnings are not given only to the mature leaders of the church but to all who call on the name of the Lord, from the least to the greatest, for Satan is no respecter of persons.

Where, then, can we find comfort when we are assaulted by temptations? Are we not aligned with Christ, who Himself faced temptation

---

1. We are indebted to *The Christian Warfare Against the Devil, World, and Flesh* by John Downame (London: William Stansby, 1634), 1–7 and 31–40 respectively, for both this and the following section.

2. Leigh, 202.

(Matt. 4)? Does temptation not confirm our place alongside the saints who are positioned against the devil on the battlefield, when instead of his kiss we feel his kick, instead of his commendation we suffer his confrontation, and instead of his flattery we face his slander? Christ says a kingdom divided against itself cannot stand. Therefore, if we find ourselves struggling against sin and vexed by Satan's assaults, let us be consoled by realizing that we have been rescued from the power of darkness and transferred into the kingdom of light. We have been delivered from the bondage of sin and yoked to Christ (Matt. 11:28).

Three Agents of Temptation

The second thing to understand about temptation is that it comes to us from three agents. Knowing this makes us more watchful and better prepared to meet it. The concentration of all efforts on a united front can be a great weakness in a military advance. A wise general supports his front line with a flank of soldiers, and, if possible, a battalion at the rear. Thus, Satan, being a crafty serpent, hopes to accomplish his coup against us with three agents of temptation.

These temptations are referred to in 1 John 2:16 as "the lust of the flesh, and the lust of the eyes, and the pride of life," all of which are not of the Father but of the world. "The lust of the flesh" refers to the sinful pleasures that life offers, "the lust of the eyes" to the riches and possessions of this world, and "the pride of life" to the honor and praise of men. All temptations to sin come from these three sources. If one source fails, Satan has another in waiting; if one weakens, he has another by which to wound.

The two great enemies that help Satan advance his temptations are the world and the flesh. Paul speaks of Satan as "the prince of the power of the air" (Eph. 2:2), meaning that the world has fallen under his power and influence. Thus, the world assaults us on all sides, offering us riches for our service, pleasures for our sinful compliance, and honor for our worship. The flesh is a worse enemy than the world, however, because it is the inborn traitor of which the apostle speaks so lamentably in Romans 7, decrying even himself as a "wretched man" (v. 24). This inner self of corruption and sinfulness, though crucified and dethroned by our new birth in Christ, is never wholly mortified in this life. This corrupted self makes us prone to sin and ready to assent to Satan's temptations. It is a traitor that claims to be for us but is really against us and allied with Satan. When we would bar the door against sin, our flesh opens the door and lets sin in. When we would resist temptation, our flesh urges us toward it, promising to satisfy our deepest lusts if we will sin "just this once." Thus, our flesh wages constant war against our Spirit-bred desires and opposes any good that we would do, whether by word, deed, thought, affection, or motive (Gal. 5:17; Rom. 7:14–23). It is the sinful desire still breathing in us that responds to every temptation, whether brought by Satan or his cohorts (James 1:14).

If these are the odds in our fight against Satan, the world, and our flesh, some might suppose that it would be better to remain asleep in Satan's dungeon than to be awakened to continual spiritual warfare. How wrong they are! Is numbness the sign of health or disease? Is perpetual sleep the sign of peace and safety or of danger and vulnerability? What does avoiding war provide but bondage to the one who wages it, namely, Satan?

When the war rages and we face an enemy we cannot see (Satan) in his own backyard (the world) with a turncoat in our breast (the flesh), we must remember that we engage in this warfare under the banner of Christ, the victorious King. Therefore, as we will soon see, we may enjoy abundant comfort and hope even in the midst of battle.

Temptations Are Subject to God's Providence

Third, temptation, like everything in this life, is subject to our heavenly Father's good and gracious providence. We have seen that afflictions are a necessary and good part of our pilgrimage. That is also true of temptations, which, at times, are nothing more than grievous afflictions. Because we belong to Christ and God is working all things to conform us to Christ's image (Rom. 8:28–29), even temptations are ordained to help us to grow in grace. Temptations cannot be outside God's decree, for Ephesians 1:11 says, He "worketh all things after the counsel of his own will," and Psalm 33:11 says, "The counsel of the LORD standeth for ever, the thoughts of his heart to all generations."[3] The Lord's own words to Peter in Luke 22:31–32 indicate that temptation is a means for growing in grace. He says, "Simon, Simon, behold, Satan hath desired to have you, that he may sift you as wheat: but I have prayed for thee, that thy faith fail not: and when thou art converted, strengthen thy brethren."

Christ did not pray that Peter would be delivered from temptation (John 17:15) because He knew it was good for Peter to face it. Though Peter was sincere in saying that he was ready to stand with the Lord, even unto death (Luke 22:33), he was unaware of two things: Satan's malicious desire to destroy him and his own weakness under trial. The Lord did not make Peter aware of these things, for that would have done him no good (v. 34). Instead, Christ enrolled Peter in the school of failure, where Peter's grievous fall taught him about the lurking adversary and his desire to devour us (1 Peter 5:8). It showed him the need to be sober-minded and prepared for action (1 Peter 1:13), the need to resist the devil with a firm faith (1 Peter 5:9), and the need to supplement faith with Christ-like qualities which, when duly practiced, keep us from falling (2 Peter 1:5–10).

Like afflictions, temptations have a sanctifying purpose within God's grand scheme to deliver us from the power and presence of sin. Like our afflictions, temptations test what we are made of, passing over us like a magnet and drawing dross to the surface. One provocation causes jealousy and anger to surface; another unearths lust; another calls pride from its hiding place; yet another awakens coveting. So while Satan plots our fall with his temptations, God ordains them for our humility. What Satan means for evil, God means for our good (Gen. 45:5; 50:20). The sin that is meant to ruin and shame us is sovereignly worked for our benefit (Acts 2:23, 36; 4:27–28). Therefore, we must sincerely and repeatedly pray the sixth petition of the Lord's Prayer, that

---

3. "God, from all eternity, did, by the most wise and holy counsel of his own will, freely, and unchangeably ordain whatsoever comes to pass: yet so, as thereby neither is God the author of sin, nor is violence offered to the will of the creatures; nor is the liberty or contingency of second causes taken away, but rather established" (Westminster Confession of Faith 3.1, "Of God's Eternal Decree").

our Heavenly Father will "lead us not into temptation, but deliver us from evil" (Matt. 6:13). We pray that God will graciously and lovingly steer us from temptations from which we would not recover except by His aid. We pray that He will protect us from the evil and malicious intent of Satan, knowing that if we should fall into sin, God will bring us to repentance and grant us renewed strength and grace.

Knowing that our heavenly Father is sovereign over temptation is a great comfort. It means that God intends our construction, not our destruction (Eph. 4:11–13), and will therefore give us sufficient grace in our temptations (2 Cor. 12:9). It means that God will not tempt us beyond what we can bear but will bring forth good from evil (1 Cor. 10:13) because He knows what falls we can bear and what falls are too much for us.[4] It means that God will not allow Satan to sift us any more than is necessary to remove our chaff and purge us of the sin that plagues us and slows our walk in Christ (Luke 22:32; Heb. 12:1–2, 11–13). In short, it means that God will use even the devil as our physician, turning his efforts into a means for healing and growth.

The apostle Paul enjoyed the comfort of this truth when he appeared before Caesar. In 2 Timothy 4:16, he tells us that no one stood by him during that time, for everyone had deserted him. Not one person pled for him, testified for him, or comforted him. Paul stood alone before the world's throne of power. Clearly Satan intended this trial to weaken the apostle and to crush him with despair. But a greater One than Satan was in charge. Paul's heavenly Father had ordained long before that this temptation of Satan would sift Paul of the chaff of trusting in man (Ps. 146:3) and would strengthen his trust in the Lord (Ps. 118:6). So Paul writes of this experience: "The Lord stood with me, and strengthened me…and I was delivered out of the mouth of the lion. And the Lord shall deliver me from every evil work, and will preserve me unto his heavenly kingdom: to whom be glory for ever and ever. Amen" (2 Tim. 4:17–18). May God grant us the same comfort in all our temptations!

Having learned that temptations are the universal experience of God's redeemed people; that temptations are the work of Satan, the

---

4. Leigh, 202.

world, or our own flesh; and that temptations are under our Father's good and loving providence, we now turn our attention to God's promises regarding temptation.

God's Promise of Strength in Temptation

The Lord promises that He will give us victory over temptation. James 4:7 says: "Submit yourselves therefore to God. Resist the devil, and he will flee from you." Were the promise limited, the verse might have said, "and he will usually flee from you," or "he may flee from you," or, worst of all, "do not resist the devil, for he will not flee from you." Despite our feeling that such limitations might be true, God's promise is unalterably true, for it is spoken by One who cannot lie (Mal. 3:6): "Resist the devil, and he will flee." If we submit to God, He promises without question that He will give us the strength to resist the devil until he flees from us, not because of who we are but because we are part of the Lord's army, and He enables us to stand firm in His power in the evil day (Eph. 6:10–11, 13).

In addition, 1 John 5:18 tells us, "We know that whosoever is born of God sinneth not; but he that is begotten of God keepeth himself, and that wicked one toucheth him not." John's point is that believers do not live in continual sin as unbelievers do because they are born of God (1 John 3:9). Therefore, believers are enabled by God's indwelling Spirit and abiding grace to keep themselves from sin. Satan cannot touch them, and they will be victorious over Satan's temptations!

Isaiah 27 promises us sustained strength in the midst of temptation. Isaiah says: "In that day the LORD with his sore and great and strong sword shall punish leviathan the piercing serpent, even leviathan that crooked serpent; and he shall slay the dragon that is in the sea. In that day sing ye unto her, A vineyard of red wine. I the LORD do keep it; I will water it every moment: lest any hurt it, I will keep it night and day" (vv. 1–3). We will be victorious over Satan because God will slay the dragon for us, and we will have strength against temptation because in it God will guard and protect us from all harm. Oh, how merciful the Lord is to give us such promises! Would that we were not so slow to believe them and draw comfort from them!

In Matthew 16:18, God offers another promise. He says, "I will build my church; and the gates of hell shall not prevail against it." That means we will have strength to withstand the enemy's assaults, no matter how long the siege or how hard the blows. Gates were a sign of a city's strength and the place where its wise counselors sat (Amos 5:15), so here the Lord promises that neither the strength nor the wisdom of Satan will prevail against us.[5] Yes, the devil is a roaring lion, but Christ is the lion of Judah. The devil is a serpent, but Christ is the bronze serpent of healing. The devil is subtle and crafty, but Christ is wisdom (1 Cor. 1:30); He teaches us to discern the wiles and subterfuges of Satan (2 Cor. 2:11; 2 Peter 2:9). The devil is strong and powerful, but God will keep us safe from all harm (Pss. 60:12; 91:4; 1 Peter 1:5).[6]

The Lord gives us strength against temptation by promising, "I will be their God, and they shall be my people" (Jer. 31:33). God promises to free us from all evil that might hurt us and to give us good things, whether temporal, spiritual, or eternal.[7] As if this were not enough to comfort us, the Lord guarantees His promise through Christ's shed blood. Hebrews 2:14–15 says Christ took on flesh so that "through death he might destroy him that had the power of death, that is, the devil; and deliver them who through fear of death were all their lifetime subject to bondage." And 1 John 4:4 says, "Greater is he that is in you, than he that is in the world." So God has taken us unto Himself and given Himself to us by His inviolable covenant. Our safety and victory over the devil are forever secure.

The same apostle who longed for the day when he would be set free from the *presence* of sin found hope in the assurance that he had already been set free from the power of sin. He could thus say, "To live is Christ" (Phil. 1:21). After crying for deliverance from bodily corruption, he could say: "I thank God through Jesus Christ our Lord. So then with the mind I myself serve the law of God" (Rom. 7:25). After rejoicing in the certain hope of a stingless death and conquered grave, he could say, "Therefore, my beloved brethren, be ye steadfast, unmov-

---

5. Ibid., 204.
6. Ibid., 203.
7. Ibid., 104.

able, always abounding in the work of the Lord, forasmuch as ye know that your labor is not in vain in the Lord" (1 Cor. 15:58). The strength to overcome sin and the devil is a *present* reality. May God help us to believe and enjoy that promise.

If we fail to use the strength the Lord provides or offer no resistance to temptation and fall into sin, what then? Does the Lord promise us anything? Yes, the Lord offers comforting words even then to us. He says He *will* have mercy and He *will* restore us.

God's Promise to Restore Us

Of all the disciples, people seem to relate most to Peter. Peter was a crude fisherman who could not control his tongue. Even so, people like Peter, probably because they identify with him—not in his fishing but in his failing. We like Peter because he failed and was restored. That gives us hope, for in Peter we see proof of God's covenant faithfulness in mercy, pardon, and restoration to one who has succumbed to temptation.

Note that our comfort rests in God's covenant faithfulness. That is the foundation of all the promises. It is where the hope and comfort of every saint is rooted. We would have no hope of God's *forgiveness* had He not covenanted to give it. In Genesis 17:7, God promises, "I will establish my covenant between me and thee and thy seed after thee in their generations for an everlasting covenant, to be a God unto thee, and to thy seed after thee." We would have no hope of God's *comfort* in our afflictions had He not covenanted to give it. Isaiah 66:13 tells us, "As one whom his mother comforteth, so will I comfort you; and ye shall be comforted in Jerusalem." We would have no assurance of *pardon* for our sins had He not promised it. Isaiah 55:7 says, "Let the wicked forsake his way, and the unrighteous man his thoughts: and let him return unto the LORD, and he will have mercy upon him; and to our God, for he will abundantly pardon." We would have no assurance of *restoration* had the Lord not promised it. Jeremiah 27:22 says, "They shall be carried to Babylon, and there shall they be until the day that I visit them, saith the LORD; then will I bring them up, and restore them to this place." What the Lord has given, we will surely possess.

When Moses asked the Lord to show His glory, the Lord said He would let His goodness pass before Moses and would proclaim His name as "The LORD" (Ex. 33:18–19). God answered this way because it was by His faithfulness to His name regarding the stiff-necked people of Israel that Moses would see His glory. In Exodus 34:6–7, the Lord proclaims His name as, "The LORD, the LORD God, merciful and gracious, longsuffering, and abundant in goodness and truth, keeping mercy for thousands, forgiving iniquity and transgression and sin." In that name is the promise to anyone who has fallen that God has chosen to glorify Himself by having mercy on the ill-deserving, pardoning the guilty, and restoring the fallen.

First, God glorifies Himself by having mercy on us. He keeps His healing waters flowing because He promised that in giving His name to us (Ex. 33:19). The Lord states His name with a declaration of power. He says, "The LORD, the LORD God," meaning He is the strong, almighty God, the One whose hands hold power. God then proclaims His mercy, grace, longsuffering, goodness, truth, and forgiveness. His almighty power is behind His mercy. Edward Leigh thus says: "He is Jehovah, always the same, unchangeable, he will not alter his love to you, and for the more assurance he repeats that title twice; then follows his power: God. Though you be weak, he is strong, merciful or compassionate towards repentant and believing sinners, and though they be unworthy yet he is gracious."[8]

God promises mercy because His name proclaims it. We must not doubt the Lord's willingness to have mercy on us when we fall into sin. We must greatly lament our falling and be humbled by it, but we must also know the Lord will have mercy on us. Leigh says, "He will show mercy, not because you are good, but because he is good; not because you can please him, but because mercy pleases him" (Micah 7:18).[9]

With this firm promise of mercy and underlying power, we may be comforted that even in our sin we do not lose His love or favor, for by His covenant He has bound Himself to look upon us through His beloved Son (Col. 3:3). God is not blind to our sins or ignorant of them. Neither is

---

8. Ibid., 214.
9. Ibid.

He like a mother who dismisses her toddler's naughtiness. Rather, Christ has sufficiently paid the penalty for our sins so that the Lord may have mercy on us when we sin and show steadfast love to us forever.

Let us, then, acquaint ourselves with some specific promises of God's mercy. Jeremiah 31:12 and 25 assure us that the Lord will have mercy, saying: "Therefore they shall come and sing in the height of Zion, and shall flow together to the goodness of the LORD…and their soul shall be as a watered garden; and they shall not sorrow any more at all…. For I have satiated the weary soul, and I have replenished every sorrowful soul." Sorrow is removed from the sin-burdened soul by God's mercy. In Romans 11:29, Paul comforts us by saying, "The gifts and calling of God are without repentance." The gifts of the covenant and our entrance into it by God's sovereign good pleasure are irrevocable because He has promised to have mercy on us. So whatever doubt or fear we have that God will not have mercy upon us is silenced by God's command to us to receive the mercy that Christ has secured for us. Hebrews 4:14 and 16 say, "Seeing then that we have a great high priest, that is passed into the heavens, Jesus the Son of God…let us therefore come boldly unto the throne of grace, that we may obtain mercy, and find grace to help in time of need." How can we doubt God's mercy when He commands us to come and receive it? Consider what Isaiah 55:7 says: "Let the wicked forsake his way, and the unrighteous man his thoughts: and let him return unto the LORD, and he will have mercy upon him." Though we multiply our sins by adding unrighteousness to wickedness, God multiplies His mercy, for He will not reward us according to our sins but according to His great mercy, which is as great as the distance between heaven and earth (Ps. 103:8–11)![10]

Second, if the Lord extends mercy to us when we fall, He also abundantly pardons us of all our sin. Isaiah 55:7 says, "Let the wicked forsake his way, and the unrighteous man his thoughts: and let him return unto the LORD, and he will have mercy upon him; and to our God, for he will abundantly pardon." Having received God's mercy, we are also assured of His full pardon. Look again at the Lord's name in Exodus 34:6–7:

---

10. Ibid., 215.

"The LORD, the LORD God, merciful and gracious, longsuffering, and abundant in goodness and truth, keeping mercy for thousands, forgiving iniquity and transgression and sin." Though we daily offend God with our sins, His name proclaims that He is longsuffering and abundant in goodness toward us. In His goodness, He is ready to bestow all the benefits of the covenant to us, which include abundant mercy and the pardon of all our sins. The Lord's name declares that He is ready to fulfill His promises to us. He begins by forgiving all our iniquity (our original corruption), all our transgression (our actual rebellion), and all our sin (sins of custom and habit). Though our sins are compounded by many degrees, we cannot commit more than God can remit, for our sins are the sins of men (Mark 3:28), while His mercy and pardon are of an infinite, eternal, and covenant-keeping God.[11]

Knowing our doubts about whether God will forgive our sin, especially when sin has long hindered us, our Lord adds His righteousness and faithfulness to our pardon. As 1 John 1:9 says, "If we confess our sins, he is faithful and just to forgive us our sins, and to cleanse us from all unrighteousness." That means God is just in forgiving our sin. While sin transgresses the law of God and therefore incurs guilt before Him, which He cannot overlook, God imputed the sin of we who are united to Christ by saving faith to Him upon the cross, where He paid the full price God's law demanded of them. Therefore, God can justly forgive and cleanse us of all unrighteousness. Oh, that we would grasp the comfort of this promise!

If we still doubt God's forgiveness of our sins, God appeals to Christ's advocacy on our behalf. In 1 John 2:1–2 we read: "My little children, these things write I unto you, that ye sin not. And if any man sin, we have an advocate with the Father, Jesus Christ the righteous: And he is the propitiation for our sins." What great comfort this is! If we sin, we know Christ is at the Father's right hand, pleading that we be forgiven of all our sins and cleansed of every stain of unrighteousness, whether in our hearts, our thoughts, our words, our deeds, our affections, or our motives. He pleads for this all-encompassing pardon because He is the

---

11. Ibid., 214–15.

propitiation for our sins and the atoning satisfaction for everything that He asks the Father to forgive. As Romans 11:33 says: "O the depth of the riches both of the wisdom and knowledge of God! How unsearchable are his judgments, and his ways past finding out!" If we imagine Christ wresting from the Father what He is unwilling to give, remember what Paul says in Romans 11:32: "God hath concluded them all in unbelief, that he might have mercy upon all." God is as pleased to pardon us as the Son is to ask it on our behalf, because it is His name to do so and it is Christ's commission to do so.

Finally, if the Lord has mercy on us and pardons all our sins, He also fully restores us. Psalm 145:14 says, "The LORD raiseth up all those that be bowed down." Jeremiah 33:6 says the Lord promises restoration to the fallen: "Behold, I will bring it health and cure, and I will cure them, and will reveal unto them the abundance of peace and truth." Luke 22:31–32 says Christ's intercession not only saved Peter from ruin but also restored his commission as a disciple to "strengthen thy brethren." What Christ did for Peter He also does for us so that He might bring many of us to glory (Heb. 2:10).[12]

Why, then, do we wait so long to confess our sin and return to the Lord? The Prodigal Son found his father waiting in the road for him (Luke 15:11–24) not only to show him mercy but also to pardon his sin and restore him to his rightful position in the family. If, then, we who are evil know how to give good gifts to our children, how much more will our heavenly Father grant us mercy, pardon, restoration, and all good things (Matt. 7:11; Luke 11:13)? "Come unto me," He says, "all ye who are heavy laden and burdened under the guilt of your sins, and I will give you rest, for I have come to seek and to save the lost and to give my life a ransom for many" (cf. Matt. 11:28; Mark 2:17; Luke 19:10; Matt. 20:28).

God's Promise of Grace in Gross Sin

If our sins do not worry us, their great number might, or their gravity, or how far they have distanced us from the Lord, or for how long. We may

---

12. Ibid., 226.

fear that we have sinned so much that we have exhausted God's store of grace and mercy, or have aroused His disgust, or have fallen beyond His reach, or have been fallen for so long that He has forgotten us.

James 4:6 shuts the mouth of all such doubts, saying, "But he giveth more grace!" Our doubts are not so great, so overwhelming, or so debilitating that they can overwhelm the Lord, for no matter how great are our sins, God gives more grace! He has more grace than all our fears, all our doubts, all our sins, and all our faithlessness. He is jealous for His name, which He has proclaimed to us and by which He has covenanted Himself to be our gracious, loving God. As Leigh says, "Though your sins were as great as idolatry in the first table, or whoredom in the second, yet God will forgive and sanctify you…[for] the sea can drown mountains as well as mole-hills."[13]

God promises that He will never leave us or forsake us (Heb. 13:5). Some might question that, saying, "I have left Him." Others might claim, "He may never leave me, but there is no guarantee that I will never leave Him." Whatever it takes, we must nail into our minds and hearts that "God's covenant is to make us faithful in His covenant; [so that while] the acts of faith and repentance are ours…the power of doing them [is] God's."[14] If there were no other promise in Scripture, we could rest our hope on these words of the Lord to Solomon: "I will dwell among the children of Israel, and will not forsake my people Israel" (1 Kings 6:13).

But the Lord has given us much more in the finished work of Christ. If the promises given before Christ's death were sufficient to save the elect of the Old Testament, how much more can we be saved who live in the days after Christ's life, death, resurrection, and intercession (Heb. 7:25)! How sure, then, are the promises that came after the cross! Therefore, rest your hope on the words of the apostle in Romans 8:32, 35–39:

> He that spared not his own Son, but delivered him up for us all, how shall he not with him also freely give us all things?… Who shall separate us from the love of Christ? shall tribulation, or distress, or persecution, or famine, or nakedness, or peril, or sword? As it is writ-

13. Ibid., 228.
14. Ibid., 219.

ten, For thy sake we are killed all the day long; we are accounted as sheep for the slaughter. Nay, in all these things we are more than conquerors through him that loved us. For I am persuaded, that neither death, nor life, nor angels, nor principalities, nor powers, nor things present, nor things to come, nor height, nor depth, nor any other creature, shall be able to separate us from the love of God, which is in Christ Jesus our Lord.

God promises to heal us even when we have backslidden and our sin is very great (Jer. 2:11–14). He will heal us completely (Jer. 3:12–15, 22). Hosea 14:4 says, "I will heal their backsliding, I will love them freely: for mine anger is turned away from him." God's anger has turned away from us because Christ, on the bloody cross, has fully satisfied the penalty of sin for us (Gal. 3:13). God can no longer be angry with us but will have mercy on us. He will pardon and restore us. Wherever sin has abounded, His grace has abounded much more unto the forgiving of all sin and the restoring of the sheep to the fold (Rom. 5:20–21).

Truths to Remember in Times of Temptation

Here is a summary of various truths that the Puritans encourage us to remember in times of temptation:

1. When you are tempted to commit a sin, remember the covenant! In it, God has bound Himself to you. This is a great comfort because the covenant of grace includes all of God's promises. It is a bundle of great and precious promises, which all begin, "I will give you...."[15] Can you knowingly and willingly sin against such grace?[16]

2. But remember, just as God has bound Himself to you, you have pledged yourself to Him. This covenant bond should therefore be a curb to committing any sin. When tempted, you should say: "No; I must not lie, swear, or break the Lord's Day; for it is against my bargain. On such a Lord's Day, in such a congregation, before such and such witnesses, I took the sacrament of baptism and pledged that by the grace of my Lord I would sin no more."[17]

15. Ibid., 107.
16. Ibid., 113.
17. Ibid.

3. When a child of God wrestles with Satan in temptation or lust, he may challenge the covenant of God's hands, and say: "Lord, hast not thou said that thou wilt deliver me out of the hands of all mine enemies? Is it not a part of thy covenant?"[18]

4. When you are tempted to sin and sincerely desire to be delivered from it, call on the Lord to deliver you according to His promise in 2 Peter 2:9, "The Lord knoweth how to deliver the godly out of temptations," and His promise in Psalm 91:3, "Surely he shall deliver thee from the snare of the fowler, and from the noisome pestilence." Memorize these verses and repeat them before God when you are tempted. Ask God to make good on His Word. In this way, these promises will be wings by which you may fly away from the tempest (Ps. 55:4–8).

5. Whenever you face temptation, consider Christ. Consider that He was tempted as you are and can sympathize with your struggle (Heb. 4:15). Consider that His suffering for you in temptation enables Him to help you in your temptation (Heb. 2:18), and that He is your victorious Captain and is not ashamed to call you brethren (Heb. 2:11). Consider that He has overcome the devil in your flesh, and that the victory of the Head is the victory of His members (Heb. 2:10). Consider that He will not suffer any to perish whom the Father has entrusted to His eternal care (John 6:37–40); that He makes intercession for you, praying specifically for you in your temptation (Luke 22:32; John 17:9a, 15); and that His intercession is the effectual prayer of a Righteous Man (James 5:16), by which He is able to save you to the uttermost (Heb. 7:25).[19]

6. When you face temptation, let Christ's promises to those who overcome temptation (Rev. 2 and 3) motivate you to resist. He has promised that those who overcome will eat of the tree of life in the paradise of God (2:7), will not be hurt by the second death (2:11), and will be given the hidden manna and a white stone with a new name (2:17). They will be given authority over nations and the morning star (2:26–28). They will be clothed in white garments, and Christ will confess their names before the Father (3:5). They will be pillars

---

18. Ibid., 204.
19. Ibid., 202–203.

in the temple of God, will have the name of God and the new Jerusalem written upon them (3:12), and will sit with Christ on His throne (3:21). What incomparable promises those are!

7. In your ongoing struggle with temptation, take heart in the sure promise of Romans 16:20, that "the God of peace shall bruise Satan under your feet shortly." The day of Satan's doom and your victory is soon to come.

8. If you fear that you are falling away from God because of your sins, remember that His counsel, upon which your salvation is founded, is sure and unchangeable (Eph. 1:4). Remember that His love for you is from everlasting and is therefore unchangeable (Jer. 31:3), and that He is able to guard you for an inheritance incorruptible, undefiled, and unfading, ready to be revealed in the last time (1 Peter 1:4–5).[20] Thus, your assurance is not in yourself but in Him. As you lay hold on Him, He will hold you fast, for as a man will not lose what he buys with his own money, so Christ will not lose you, whom He purchased with His own blood (Acts 20:28).[21]

9. When you fall, remember that the Lord knows those who are His, and even if you are faithless, He will remain faithful to you (2 Tim. 2:13, 19).

10. When you are overtaken by temptation, remember that it does not matter how much it wounds you, for Christ is the Great Physician who will heal you and restore your strength.[22]

11. If you are guilty of a multitude of sins, remember that God has a greater multitude of mercies, according to His promise in Romans 5:20.[23] Believe with David that those mercies are for you, and call upon Him as he did (Ps. 51:1).

12. Remember that neither the foulness of sin, nor the multitude of sin, nor long continuance in sin can prejudice His goodness.[24]

---

20. Ibid., 225.
21. Ibid., 226.
22. Ibid., 228.
23. Ibid.
24. Ibid., 214.

13. Meditate much upon Ezekiel 34:16, which says, "I will seek that which was lost, and bring again that which was driven away, and will bind up that which was broken, and will strengthen that which was sick." Christ is the Good Shepherd who keeps watch over your soul. If you are lost, He will find you. If you have been driven away by any violence of temptation, He will bring you back. If sin or lust has wounded your heart, He will bind you up, for He has promised to make you faithful in His covenant, and He will surely do it.[25]

14. Be careful not to measure your humiliation and sorrow for sin against that of another. In the wisdom of God, "not all are afflicted with the same violence, though all be sick of the same disease."[26] Some lie under the fever and rage of despair, while others are sick to the stomach over the bitterness of their sins. Some lie on the bed of sorrow over sin, while others feel themselves to be on a rack of horror. Look more at the quality of your sorrow than at the quantity of it; test it by the touchstone of truth rather than weighing it on a balance of comparison.[27]

15. What, then, is true humiliation? What is the godly sorrow that leads to repentance (2 Cor. 7:10)? True sorrow for sin drives a sinner utterly out of himself. It stirs up a vehement thirst for Christ and a settled resolution to cleave wholly to Him as Lord, Savior, King, and Priest. Can you attest to such sorrow? Then believe it to be true and cleave to Christ. Do not compare yourself with another.[28]

16. Remember that the way God speaks peace to your heart and makes good His promises of forgiveness is by your repentance (Acts 2:38). Until your repentance is renewed, the comfort of His pardon is suspended (Matt. 3:7–10).[29]

17. When you confess your sin to the Lord, remember His promise in Micah 7:19, for "things that are cast into the bottom of the sea never come to sight again, but are more surely buried than things that are hid in the grave and in the bowels of the earth, which may possibly

---

25. Ibid., 219.
26. Spurstowe, 122.
27. Ibid., 121–25.
28. Ibid., 127–28.
29. Ibid., 185.

be digged out again."[30] Truly the Lord would have you know that your sins are forever forgiven and forgotten.

18. When you fall into gross sin and feel you have distanced yourself from God, you must honestly censure yourself for it. If you do not, you will never fully recover from it. An honest censure of gross sin and backsliding includes the following:[31]

a. Acknowledging that your sin merits death (Rom. 6:23), even though the grace of pardon prevents it from being inflicted upon you. Peter wept bitterly over his sin because he knew it deserved no less than death (Luke 22:62).

b. Acknowledging your unworthiness to receive God's unconditional covenant love. The Prodigal Son thus returned to his father, confessing that he was no longer worthy to be considered a son (Luke 15:21).

c. Not laying hold on God's promise of forgiveness before you renew your repentance and are thoroughly ashamed of your sin. How true is your repentance if you are not sincerely sorry for and ashamed of yourself on account of your sin? "To be guilty of great sins and at the same time without remorse and grief of heart to lay hold on the promises of mercy is not the acting of faith, but of presumption."[32]

d. Acknowledging that the temporal afflictions and chastisements God lays upon you for your sin are justly deserved and righteously inflicted (Isa. 57:17; 63:10; Heb. 12:5–6). Your comfort under such rods is that they do not come from God as your enemy, but from God as your provoked Father. Therefore, they are not destructive but medicinal; not a menace but a friend. Both a judge and a physician may cut off a man's hand, but the former will do it to satisfy justice while the latter will cut off a diseased limb to save the rest of the body.

---

30. Ibid., 192.
31. Ibid., 180–88.
32. Ibid., 185.

19. Be careful not to censure yourself too much, for the purpose of censure is not to lead you to despair but to work true repentance in your heart.[33] In this, heed the following:

a. Do not conclude that you have fallen from the state of justification and the grace of adoption. "The love of God in Christ is an endless and unchangeable love (John 13:1), and its perpetuity is founded not upon anything in us, but upon the firm rock of his will and counsel."[34] A fall into gross sin will breach your justification and adoption by withholding their comforts and privileges, but your right to those comforts and privileges by repentance is in no way extinguished. To be under the power of an interdiction is not the same as to be under the power of an ejection. Like Absalom when he returned to Jerusalem, you may not enjoy the countenance of the King's face for a time, but you are not in permanent exile (2 Sam. 14:24).[35]

b. Do not conclude that the pardon of your former sins is voided by your present sin. The commission of new sins does not revoke the pardon of former sins or make the guilt of former sins return, no more than subsequent debt makes former payments void (Isa. 44:22). "For God, when he pardons, does not insert any conditional clauses that carry a respect to our future conversation.... His gifts and graces are the fruits of his immutable counsel and will and [are] therefore without all repentance."[36]

c. Do not conclude that you have lost all sanctifying grace. Grievous sins may put you into a spiritual coma, but they do not reduce you to a carcass. They may blast and wither your precious fruits of grace and profession, but they do not wholly destroy the root and seed from which those grow. The seed of God still abides in you and you will again bring forth the fruits of repentance (1 John 3:9). God has put His fear into your heart so that you will not turn from Him (Jer. 32:40), for "He that keeps us by faith keeps faith itself in us."[37]

---

33. Ibid., 188–96.
34. Ibid., 189.
35. Ibid.
36. Ibid., 191.
37. Ibid., 193.

    d. Do not conclude that you shall never enjoy any comfort again. Such a conclusion runs contrary to the promises of mercy God has made to penitent sinners (Jer. 3:12–14), as well as to many men in Scripture such as David and Peter, whom God comforted after they fell and honored with renewed service. Remember the promise the Lord made to repenting Israel in Zephaniah 3:19–20: "Behold, at that time I will undo all that afflict thee: and I will save her that halteth, and gather her that was driven out; and I will get them praise and fame in every land where they have been put to shame. At that time will I bring you again, even in the time that I gather you: for I will make you a name and a praise among all people of the earth, when I turn back your captivity before your eyes, saith the LORD."

20. Finally, draw comfort from the truth that in his every attempt to force the Lord to cast you off, Satan is "kicking against the goads" (Zech. 3:1–5). Satan cannot hurt you or trip you because the keeping power of the King of kings is incontestable. The Lord will either keep you from falling or restore you if you fall, for it is His name to do so.

Imagine that the devil sends one of his imps to find a way to force the Lord to break His covenant with you and to count you unworthy of His love, mercy, grace, and promises. The imp would surely return to Satan with this report: "I can find no way to do what you wish, for the King's *love* for them is unconditional. His love is not based on anything in them at all. He knows they are not worthy of it, and yet He sets His love upon them. His *mercy* also has no limits. No matter how many times they fall, He forgives them as if it were the first time. No matter how far they fall, even to the very brink of hell, His arm of salvation reaches them and restores them to their place. As for His *grace*, it is like a bottomless treasure chest tipped over for them. Whenever they have need, He offers them His glorious and inexhaustible riches through his own Son. His store is almighty, no matter their need, and all-sufficient, no matter how great their need. And what can I say of His *promises*! These are the very tether by which He moors them to Himself. In His precious and very great promises, He guarantees them His unconditional love, His bottomless ocean of mercy, and His inexhaustible grace in His Son. I can only say that, of all people and nations of the earth, blessed are those whose hope is in the promises of God!"

Study Questions

1. Read Romans 7:14–25. As believers, why will we struggle against sin until our dying day? What relief do God's promises afford us in the midst of these struggles?

2. When you are tempted by some lust of the flesh, why does Satan try to convince you that you are the only one struggling with this temptation?

3. Read 1 John 2:15–17. List some ways you can fight against your lustful flesh, lustful eyes, and ungodly pride. To whom, above all, should you resort when assaulted by temptations? Why?

4. How does God use even our temptations to sanctify and mature our faith? How does this comfort us?

5. What does James 4:7 say provides us strength in temptation? What other texts in Scripture assure believers that Christ and His promises are stronger than Satan and all his temptations?

6. What promises have you leaned hardest on when confronted with temptation? Have you shared these promises and what they mean to you with others? If not, why not? If so, when?

7. Read Exodus 34:6–7. How can God's very names serve as promises? How can you make more use of Christ's names for your own spiritual strength, comfort, and perseverance?

8. How does Micah 7:18 reveal God in Christ as a God of mercy? Have you learned to plead upon God's mercy? If so, what fruits has that worked out in your life? If not, why not?

9. Read Luke 15:11–24. If God is as merciful as the prodigal's father and promises to forgive the sins of all who flee penitently and trustingly to Him, why are we prone to delay before confessing our sin and returning to the Lord?

10. A friend tells you he has fallen into adultery. He is grieved over his sin and has broken off the adulterous relationship, but he does not know how to approach God. What would you advise him?

Using God's Promises in Fighting Sin

We have seen how easy it is to relate to Peter because he fell into grievous sin (Luke 22:54–62) and was graciously restored (John 21:15–19). Yet we also empathize with Paul, whose gigantic faith greatly encourages us to trust God to be faithful to us, no matter how great the opposition. Paul's epistles dominate the New Testament with instructions on all matters of the gospel and call us to live out our mystical union with Christ. Then, too, we think of the deep pit from which God delivered Paul, who persecuted the early church. He was without equal in his opposition to the new teaching of the Lord's disciples, but then Christ saved him, rescuing His strongest opponent and making him His strongest advocate. Paul never forgot the great chasm across which the Lord's arm of salvation had stretched to redeem him. He thereafter called himself "the chief of sinners" and heralded his conversion as God's means of assuring others that He is willing to save anyone (1 Tim. 1:12–16).

However, the primary reason why most of us like Paul is that his struggle with sin, which he related in Romans 7:14–25, is so true of our own experience. Just when we find it impossible to put into words how frustrated we are in our struggle with the flesh, we see how clearly Paul expresses that struggle. Just when we think no one understands our struggle to die to sin and live to God, we see how Paul understands it perfectly. Paul seems to know us better than we know ourselves, but it is really the Lord who knows Paul and us, and who graciously ordained that Paul's struggle would be infallibly recorded for our comfort and growth in grace. If Peter gives us hope because his life reveals proof of

God's mercy, forgiveness, and restoration of those who have fallen into sin, Paul gives us comfort in revealing the encouraging proof of God's sanctifying work in His people. His life also shows that our struggle with sin is not inconsistent with a state of grace but is the very evidence of it.

To see why God is willing to dwell in our hearts by His Spirit and is committed to sanctify us, we need look no further than the covenant of grace.

God Promises His Spirit[1]

Ezekiel 36:25–27 describes God's sovereign work of regeneration. In this verse, the Lord says: "Then I will sprinkle clean water upon you, and ye shall be clean: from all your filthiness, and from all your idols, will I cleanse you. A new heart also will I give you, and a new spirit will I put within you: and I will take away the stony heart out of your flesh, and I will give you an heart of flesh. And I will put my spirit within you." The New Testament parallels this promise in Christ's declaration to Nicodemus in John 3:5: "Verily, verily, I say unto thee, Except a man be born of water and of the Spirit, he cannot enter into the kingdom of God."

Regeneration is the sovereign work of God whereby He effects so radical a change in us that it can be likened only to being born again. This change of disposition is radical; before, we were inclined to all kinds of sin and uncleanness (Eph. 2:1–3; 4:17–19), but now we want to put off all corrupt ways so we may walk in righteousness and holiness (Eph. 4:20–32; Rom. 6:8–14). Our heart is changed; we previously had a stony heart (Ezek. 36:26; Mark 4:16–17), but now we have a heart of flesh (Mark 4:20). Our mind is also changed; before, our understanding was darkened and blinded by unbelief (Eph. 4:17–18; 2 Cor. 4:3–4), but now we have the mind of Christ and therefore understand the things freely given to us by God (1 Cor. 2:9–16). This change is so pervasive that Paul says, "Therefore if any man be in Christ, he is a new creature: old things are passed away; behold, all things are become new" (2 Cor.

---

1. We are indebted to *The Work of the Holy Spirit* by the Puritan-minded Octavius Winslow (London: Banner of Truth, 1972) for much of this section.

5:17). Once we were dead, but now we have come alive. As Ephesians 2:4–5 says, "But God, who is rich in mercy, for his great love wherewith he loved us, even when we were dead in sins, hath quickened us together with Christ."

These changes are the necessary consequences of the foundational act that precedes them all, namely, the triumphal entry of the Spirit of the living God into our hearts. God's regeneration of a person is nothing other than His taking possession of that person's heart to make it His dwelling place and His temple (Eph. 2:22). Because of our fall in Adam, our hearts are full of sin and uncleanness, stone cold in matters of religion, blind to truth, in bondage to sin, and dead in sin. We resist all overtures of grace, all offers of the gospel, and all calls to repent. But everything changes when the Holy Spirit takes possession of those hearts that, in eternity past, the Father elected and, in the fullness of time, Jesus Christ purchased through His life, death, and resurrection. The Spirit conquers the strong man (Mark 3:27), subdues the enemy (Rom. 8:7), softens the heart (Ezek. 36:26), bends the will (Ps. 110:3), implants a desire for Christ, and stirs a welcome response to His gospel call (Phil. 2:13), which then become evident as the heart embraces Christ by faith and turns from sin in true repentance (Acts 20:20–21; 1 Thess. 1:9).

This regeneration, or taking eternal possession of a heart by His Spirit, is what God has promised us in the covenant of grace. Ezekiel 36:27 says, "I will put my spirit within you," but notice the full context. Why will God fill His people with His Spirit? Is it because they deserve it? No. The Lord will do it for His own name's sake, that is, for the sake of His covenant by which He placed His name on His chosen ones and promised to be their eternal God and to make them His eternal people (Ex. 34:5–8). The promise of the covenant, which God made to Abraham in Genesis 17:7–8, is then repeated immediately after the promise of the Spirit: "And ye shall be my people, and I will be your God" (v. 28).

Furthermore, note how the Lord's words hem in the great promise of His Spirit's sanctifying indwelling:

> And when they entered unto the heathen, whither they went, they
> profaned my holy name, when they said to them, These are the people

of the LORD, and are gone forth out of his land. But I had pity for mine holy name, which the house of Israel had profaned among the heathen, whither they went. Therefore say unto the house of Israel, Thus saith the Lord God; I do not this for your sakes, O house of Israel, but for mine holy name's sake, which ye have profaned among the heathen, whither ye went. And I will sanctify my great name, which was profaned among the heathen, which ye have profaned in the midst of them; and the heathen shall know that I am the LORD, saith the Lord God, when I shall be sanctified in you before their eyes…. Not for your sakes do I this, saith the Lord God, be it known unto you: be ashamed and confounded for your own ways, O house of Israel (Ezek. 36:20–23, 32).

Despite His people's sin, the Lord will be faithful to the covenant He made with Abraham and all his spiritual seed (Rom. 9:6–8).

The gift of the Spirit as a fundamental part of God's covenant is also evident in New Testament references to Him as the "Spirit of promise."[2] In Galatians 3, the apostle declares that we who have believed in Jesus Christ have received "the promise of the Spirit" made to Abraham when God ratified the covenant of grace (v. 14; cf. Gen. 15). In Ephesians 1:13, Paul also calls the Holy Spirit "that holy Spirit of promise."

The promise of His Spirit is the root of everything God promises to accomplish in us by redemption. The Spirit indwells us to accomplish all that God purposed in His election of us and all that Christ purchased in His mediation for us. Without the indwelling of His Spirit, we could enjoy no other spiritual blessings, for they are the fruits of His residence within us. In giving His Spirit to us in such a personal and abiding way, God has guaranteed the perfect, irreversible, and eternal accomplishment of His electing purpose: that we might be His children, holy and without blemish at His coming (Eph. 1:5; 5:27; 1 John 3:2).

Let us comfort ourselves, then, with references to the Holy Spirit's dwelling in our hearts by faith, such as: "But ye are not in the flesh, but in the Spirit, if so be that the Spirit of God dwell in you…. But if the Spirit of him that raised up Jesus from the dead dwell in you, he that raised up Christ from the dead shall also quicken your mortal bodies by the Spirit that dwelleth in you" (Rom. 8:9, 11); "Know ye not that ye

---

2. Leigh, 247.

are the temple of God, and that the Spirit of God dwelleth in you?...
For the temple of God is holy, which temple ye are" (1 Cor. 3:16–17);
"For ye are the temple of the living God; as God hath said, I will dwell
in them" (2 Cor. 6:16); "Now therefore ye are no more strangers and
foreigners, but fellow citizens with the saints, and of the household of
God...builded together for an habitation of God through the Spirit"
(Eph. 2:19, 22); and "Ye also, as lively stones, are built up a spiritual
house" (1 Peter 2:5).

God Promises Sanctification by His Spirit

Since God promises and secures the indwelling of His Holy Spirit, the
necessary consequence is that He promises and secures our sanctification. God cannot dwell in our hearts by His Holy Spirit without
renovating and purifying it with His holy influence.

Look again at Ezekiel 36. To the promise of the Spirit's indwelling, the Lord attaches its purpose, which is our sanctification. Verse
27 says, "I will put my spirit within you, and *cause* you to walk in my
statutes, and ye shall keep my judgments, and do them."[3] This promise is repeated in Ezekiel 11:19–20, which is then repeated in the New
Testament in Hebrews 8:10 and 10:16, which tell us that God's laws are
written on our hearts and minds (cf. Jer. 31:33) by the Spirit's indwelling. Repetition indicates that this promise is of great significance (cf.
Ex. 34:6), and three-time repetition demands all our attention (cf. Isa.
6:3). What, then, can be said about a promise that is repeated multiple
times in both Old and New Testaments? Surely the Lord thereby offers
the greatest possible ground upon which to believe and draw comfort
regarding the truth of His promise of our sanctification.

These verses are solid ground for our hope in God's work in us for
His sake. Exodus 19:6 says, "And ye shall be unto me a kingdom of priests,
and an holy nation. These are the words which thou shalt speak unto the
children of Israel." Exodus 31:13 declares, "My Sabbaths ye shall keep:
for it is a sign between me and you throughout your generations; that ye

---

3. Emphasis added.

may know that I am the LORD that doth sanctify you." John 17:19 says, "And for their sakes I sanctify myself, that they also might be sanctified through the truth." First Corinthians 1:30 proclaims, "But of him are ye in Christ Jesus, who of God is made unto us wisdom, and righteousness, and sanctification, and redemption." And 1 Thessalonians 5:23–24 says: "And the very God of peace sanctify you wholly; and I pray God your whole spirit and soul and body be preserved blameless unto the coming of our Lord Jesus Christ. Faithful is he that calleth you, who also will do it." How can we doubt a promise that is repeated so often?

After establishing that God has promised our sanctification in the covenant of grace, Edward Leigh draws this conclusion: "The substance of which covenant is this, that all their sins shall be forgiven, and both the guilt and punishment thereof wholly removed. Their persons shall be justified, and their natures sanctified; the laws of God and his promises shall be written in their minds, so that they shall have the knowledge of them: and in their hearts, so that they shall have the comfort, feeling, and fruition of them: they shall not only have interest in all God's graces and blessings, but according to their need, shall have the use and enjoyment thereof."[4]

While the Spirit's triumphal entry into and permanent residence in our hearts is the occasion for our sanctification, we must understand that He performs this great work by uniting us to Christ.[5] He does this initially and permanently in our regeneration, but also throughout life in our Christian walk. The Spirit Himself is the bond of our mystical union with Christ, for it is by Him that Christ imparts holiness to us from His own holiness. Without the indwelling Spirit of God, we could have no fruition of Christ; but with the Spirit, we enjoy true spiritual union with Christ and all His graces as our Mediator, Redeemer, Savior, Lord, Prophet, Priest, and King.

This union is verified by various Scripture passages, such as John 14:20: "At that day ye shall know that I am in my Father, and ye in me,

---

4. Leigh, 300.

5. We are indebted to *The Gospel Mystery of Sanctification* by Walter Marshall (repr., Grand Rapids: Reformation Heritage Books, 1999) for this brief summary of our mystical union with Christ.

and I in you"; Ephesians 5:30–33: "For we are members of his body, of his flesh, and of his bones…and [Christ and the church] shall be one flesh"; 1 Corinthians 12:13: "For by one Spirit we are all baptized into one body, whether we be Jews or Gentiles, whether we be bond or free; and have been all made to drink into one Spirit"; and Ephesians 1:22–23: "[God] gave [Christ] to be the head over all things to the church, which is his body, the fullness of him that filleth all in all." Our union with Christ is also symbolized in several ways. John 15 describes Christ as the vine and us as the branches. Just as branches live in the vine, nourished by its living sap, so we live in Christ, drawing nourishment from His life-giving Spirit (vv. 4–5). John 6 symbolizes Christ as bread and us as those who eat Him. Just as physical bread nourishes the physical body, so Christ the living bread nourishes our spirits. Jesus says we have no life in us unless we "eat the flesh of the Son of man, and drink his blood" (v. 53).

Being united with Christ in regeneration, we necessarily share in His death to sin and resurrection to new life. Romans 6:6–8 and 11 says: "Knowing this, that our old man is crucified with him, that the body of sin might be destroyed, that henceforth we should not serve sin. For he that is dead is freed from sin. Now if we be dead with Christ, we believe that we shall also live with him…. Likewise reckon ye also yourselves to be dead indeed unto sin, but alive unto God through Jesus Christ our Lord." In other words, our union with Christ, which the Holy Spirit effects in our regeneration, means we have died with Christ (Rom. 6:6; Gal. 5:24; 6:14) to the reign and tyranny of sin (Rom. 6:12–14). We have also been raised with Christ (Eph. 2:5) so that we are alive to God (Rom. 6:11) and created anew in Christ Jesus "unto good works, which God hath before ordained that we should walk in them" (Eph. 2:10). It is no wonder, then, that Romans 8:29 describes our sanctification as being "conformed to the image of his Son." Our union with Christ results in our perfect conformity to Him. He changes us into His image, in which we have a saving interest (Rom. 8:10–11).

This union with Christ as it relates to our sanctification is of critical importance. It is from Christ and His perfect holiness (John 8:29) that we have our holiness, though it is ever imperfect in this life. His holiness is the root of our daily sanctification, resulting in the fruit of ever-increasing holiness. If we lose sight of this, we may erroneously strive after a holiness of our own making, a holiness that begins in regeneration but is perfected by our own efforts and will power; a holiness that Christ initiates by pardon but we perfect by self-wrought good works. Such thinking is contrary to the clear teaching of Scripture. It is also an impediment to the comfort that flows to us from the promise that our sanctification is a gift of the covenant that His Spirit establishes, nourishes, and perfects in us.

Therefore, as we consider the spiritual graces that are necessary for our sanctification, let us remember that they are not promised to those who work for them or are worthy of them but to those who are united to Christ by faith. From the weakest Christian to the most mature, none can boast of a holiness other than what he has received (Gal. 5:24; Rom. 8:9–15), of acceptance with God other than what he enjoys by union with Christ (Rom. 5:1–2; Eph. 1:6), and of a life of practical, daily godliness other than what Christ does in him by His indwelling Spirit (Gal. 2:20; 1 Cor. 15:10; Phil. 2:12–13).

God Promises Graces for Our Sanctification

To assure us that He will sanctify us and conform us to Christ's image, God promises us every spiritual grace that is necessary to perform the work. He can do this because the graces of His Spirit are inseparable from the Spirit Himself. Having His Spirit within us, we enjoy these graces as a necessary part of God's sovereign work in sanctifying us. These blessings flow out of us as rivers of living water, animating us and helping us to die to sin and increase in righteousness. God has not promised us an access to holiness, but holiness itself. Let us now consider several of the graces that directly relate to our struggle against sin.

God Promises Us Faith

We begin with faith, which Leigh says is a supernatural gift of God in the mind, whereby we know, apprehend, and apply the saving promise of Christ (John 3:16; Rom. 10:11) along with all promises that depend upon it (2 Cor. 1:20–21).[6] By faith, the mother of all other graces, we are united to Christ in salvation and receive all spiritual blessings (Eph. 1:3). Without faith, we remain outside of Christ and therefore are condemned: "He that believeth on him is not condemned: but he that believeth not is condemned already, because he hath not believed in the name of the only begotten Son of God…he that believeth not the Son shall not see life; but the wrath of God abideth on him" (John 3:18, 36).

God has promised faith to all whom He means to save.[7] In Philippians 1:29, Paul says, "For unto you it is given in the behalf of Christ… to believe on him." Hebrews 12:2 refers to Jesus as the Author of our faith. In Romans 12:3, Paul declares that "God hath dealt to every man the measure of faith." And in John 6:37, Jesus assures us that "all that the Father giveth me [i.e. by election] shall come to me [by faith]."[8] Christ's meaning is clear from the preceding context in which "coming to Him" is synonymous with "believing on Him" (v. 35). This promise also agrees with the offer of salvation Christ gave in Matthew 11:28: "Come unto me, all ye that labour and are heavy laden, and I will give you rest."

What if we lack such faith? There is only one thing to do—we must go to Christ! Our need for faith gives us the right to make use of God's promises, because they are made for those who need them.[9] Furthermore, awareness of our need ought to make us press Christ hard for His gift, as did the woman of Canaan in Mark 7:24–30.[10] She was deeply aware of her need and knew that only Christ could supply it. She refused to be denied its fulfillment, for she knew that Christ would not deny her. We have nothing to commend us to Christ but our need and His call for us to come to Him. Why would we refuse His call?[11]

If we are aware of our need of faith and know that without it we will perish, we ought to press hard, knock loudly, ask importunately, and wait as long as necessary for it, for the Lord has never denied anyone who came to Him. John 6:37 says, "And him that cometh to me I will

---

6. Leigh, 305.
7. Ibid.
8. Ibid.
9. Gray, 138.
10. Ibid.
11. Ibid., 141.

in no wise cast out." Therefore, if we lack faith, either to embrace Christ or to embrace His promises, let us cry out to Him as the father in Mark 9:24 did: "Help thou mine unbelief"! The Lord *will* hear and answer us, for He requires nothing of us but what He Himself gives to us.[12] He requires faith and yet He gives it; He requires repentance and yet He gives it; He requires us to come and buy and yet He asks no money; He requires us to be hungry and thirsty for Him and He makes us aware of it. Come, then, to Christ for faith, for He will freely give it to you.

Faith is necessary in our struggle against sin, for only by faith in Christ can we overcome sin. We must have saving faith in Christ or else we remain dead in sin (Eph. 2:1) and in bondage to its tyranny (John 8:34). If we trust Christ, He enables us to live by faith in our daily struggles against sin so we might experience victory in tangible ways. Hebrews 12:1–2 tells us we are able to lay aside even our besetting sins because Christ is the Author and Finisher of our faith. John also assures us of that in 1 John 5:4–5: "For whatsoever is born of God overcometh the world: and this is the victory that overcometh the world, even our faith. Who is he that overcometh the world, but he that believeth that Jesus is the Son of God?" We are given the power to overcome the world, which is dominated by sin and under the power of the father of lies, not simply by faith, but by faith in Jesus, the Son of God, who came to destroy the works of the devil (1 John 3:8). Christ, who has defeated the devil and delivered us from his power (Col. 2:15; Heb. 2:14–15), enables us to enjoy that victory, not only in eternity, but in our present everyday lives (Rom. 7:24–25).

God Promises Us Hope
Hope is the grace of God that enables us to patiently wait for the Lord to perform His promises, especially regarding redemption and eternal life.[13] It lives in expectation of those things that faith believes are promised by God.[14] Leigh says faith is the foundation of hope, while hope

12. Ibid.
13. Ibid., 310, quoting William Perkins.
14. Ibid., quoting John Calvin.

nourishes faith; faith apprehends the promises of things to come, and hope expects the things promised.[15]

How easily we give up hope! This is because our hopes are usually based on people. Our expectations depend on people's faithfulness, truthfulness, consistency, and integrity, and those are the very virtues that fallen people cannot deliver. We assume better things of people than they can give. That does not mean that we should give up hope, however, or that hoping is wrong. It means, rather, that we must place our hope no longer "in the son of man, in whom there is no help" (Ps. 146:3), but in the Lord, who is our refuge. As Psalm 146:5 says, "Happy is he that hath the God of Jacob for his help, whose hope is in the LORD his God."

God promised us hope when He promised to give us Himself. In the covenant, He said, "I will establish my covenant between me and thee and thy seed after thee in their generations for an everlasting covenant, to be a God unto thee, and to thy seed after thee" (Gen. 17:7). That promise engenders hope because it is an everlasting promise that will stand fast all our days and all the days of our seed. But notice that God promises to be our God, which is the same as promising that He will be the cause of our hope. Moreover, His Word will be the ground of our hope and His character will sustain our hope (Ps. 146:5).

This gift of hope is also evident in the words of David in Psalm 22:9, "Thou didst make me hope when I was upon my mother's breasts," as well as in the words of Paul in Colossians 1:27, "Christ in us is the hope of glory." Hope is a gift God gives to those whom He calls to Himself. He plants hope in our breasts by persuading us that He will make good on all His promises. That is why hoping in God and having God for our help are so often linked in Scripture (Ps. 146:5; Lam. 3:24–26; Ps. 14:7).[16]

While God gives us hope, His Word, specifically His promises, is the foundation of that hope. What grounds do we have for hope if not the promises of God, which are His signature or guarantee? In Psalm 119:49, David confessed that God's Word was the ground of his hope. Having God's promises in hand sustained David through all his trials though everything spoke of his ruin.

---

15. Ibid.
16. Ibid., 311.

Finally, because God gives us hope and grounds that hope in His Word, His character, specifically His attributes, sustains our hope. David said that man was happy who had the God of Jacob for his help and whose hope was in the LORD his God (Ps. 146:5). He was happy because of the sure character of God, who proves good and faithful to all His promises.

Four attributes of God sustain our hope.[17] First, our hope abides because of God's free grace. The same grace that moved God to make the covenant promise will move Him to accomplish it (1 Peter 1:13). Second, our hope abides because of God's infinite power. We know that He is able to do what He has promised (Rom. 4:20–21). Third, our hope abides because of God's infallible truth. We know that not a word of what He has promised will fall to the ground (2 Tim. 2:13). Fourth, our hope is sustained by His unsearchable wisdom. We know that God knows best when to fulfill a promise and which fulfillments will be best for His glory and for our hope. The One who has made promises to us has made Himself the foundation of all our hopes, and the One who has committed Himself to care for us is the infinite, eternal, and unchangeable God. He is the Creator of heaven and earth, the Lord and Savior of sinners. Our certain and abiding hope is in what the Lord promises to give us and sustain in us.

In our struggle against sin, God has promised to sanctify us. Look again at those promises in which the Lord has declared His commitment to forgive us of all our sins, cause us to walk in His statutes, and make us faithful to the end of our days. It is upon these promises that we hope! They are the promises of an infinite and all-powerful God, an eternal and unchanging God, a God who has bound Himself by covenant to keep His Word and accomplish all His good pleasure. As it is impossible that these promises should fail, so it is unreasonable that our hope should ever falter. We have the word of our God that He will bring the good work He began in us to completion at the day of Christ's appearing (Phil. 1:6), when He will return to save those who await Him (Heb. 9:28). Christ our Savior will present us to the Father without spot

17. Ibid., 312.

or blemish (Eph. 5:27), and will keep us from falling until then (Jude 24–25). Our hope is that we will overcome sin, dying to it more and more. God causes this hope, His Word grounds it, and His unchangeable character sustains it.

God Promises Us Obedience

One reason we relate to Paul is that his struggle to obey, recounted in Romans 7:14–25, mirrors our own experience. It is true that as Christians we are indwelt by the Spirit of holiness and therefore can actually obey. Our bondage to sin is broken and we are yoked to Christ, who always does what pleases the Father (John 8:29). Our regeneration has changed our inability to not sin (Gen. 6:5) to an ability to please God (Col. 3:8–10). But it is also true that we are still plagued by the presence of the old man.

Thus, while God has put off the old man of sin from us and put upon us the Lord Jesus Christ (Col. 3:3), we must constantly put off the old man (Col. 3:8) of disobedience and put on the Lord Jesus Christ (Col. 3:12) in daily acts of obedience. As we are "hid with Christ in God" (Col. 3:3), we are dead to sin and alive to righteousness. We have full possession of all spiritual blessings in Christ, including holiness (Eph. 1:3), but in this life, we are still plagued with the remnants of the old nature, so our reception and enjoyment of those blessings is still imperfect in both measure and degree.[18] Just as our enjoyment of Christ is partial until faith becomes sight (1 John 3:2), so our deliverance from our sinful state is partial until we put off the body of this death (Rom. 7:24–25). What hopes, then, can we have for obedience?

God has promised in His covenant to make us able to obey Him. Ezekiel 36:27 says, "And I will put my spirit within you, and cause you to walk in my statutes, and ye shall keep my judgments, and do them." Though we cannot obey perfectly in this life because of our residual sin, God has promised to conform us to Christ's image (Rom. 8:29) and thereby enable us to die more and more to sin and live more and more to righteousness. The direction of our lives, therefore, is ever-upward

---

18. Marshall, 167.

toward perfection, though mixed with some downward and even backward movement (Eccl. 7:20).

Some may object that innumerable imperatives of the epistles argue against God's making us holy and instead support the teaching that our holiness before God is acquired and self-wrought. That would mean obedience is a command rather than a gift. But the truth of what we have asserted can easily be vindicated with a single determinative context.

That obedience is commanded is clear. Romans 6:12–13 says: "Let not sin therefore reign in your mortal body, that ye should obey it in the lusts thereof. Neither yield ye your members as instruments of unrighteousness unto sin: but yield yourselves unto God, as those that are alive from the dead, and your members as instruments of righteousness unto God." On what basis does the apostle give such a command? Surely he does not believe man is able in himself to obey, for he has already given over all men to sin (Rom. 3:9–20) and would not contradict that truth here. Neither does he believe that we are able in ourselves to obey, for the very point of Romans 6:1–11 is that just as our union with Christ's death has freed us from sin's dominion, so our union with Christ's resurrection has freed us to obey. Therefore, our holiness cannot even be considered outside of Christ, in whom we enjoy it. Holiness, or obedience to God's imperatives, is not something we enjoy because of Christ, but rather something we enjoy in and from Christ (Rom. 6:11–12). Our acceptance before God is therefore *in* Him (Eph. 1:6) and not *because of* Him. The latter viewpoint suggests that Christ brings us to a place of holiness by which we can stand before God on our own, while the former states that Christ, by redemption, so unites us to Himself as the beloved of God that we stand before God in Him.

The conclusion is that obedience is commanded of God's people because it is given by Him. We obey the imperatives of the gospel because we enjoy the indicatives of the gospel. That is why the word *therefore* is often associated with the imperatives, which command obedience. Consider the following examples: "Let not sin *therefore* reign in your mortal body" (Rom. 6:12). Why? Because "our old man is crucified with him, that the body of sin might be destroyed, that henceforth we should not serve sin" (Rom. 6:6). "As ye have *therefore* received Christ

Jesus the Lord, so walk ye in him" (Col. 2:6). How did they receive Christ Jesus the Lord? With a steadfast faith (Col. 2:5). "Mortify *therefore* your members which are upon the earth; fornication, uncleanness, inordinate affection, evil concupiscence, and covetousness, which is idolatry" (Col. 3:5). Why? Because "ye [are] risen with Christ…ye are dead, and your life is hid with Christ in God" (Col 3:1, 3).

Again and again, we find that our sanctification (increasingly dying to sin and living to righteousness) rests solely and perpetually on the work of Christ and our union with Him, so that our obedience is the fruit of Christ's work in us by His Spirit. Take those familiar words of the apostle as final proof: "Wherefore, my beloved, as ye have always obeyed, not as in my presence only, but now much more in my absence, work out your own salvation with fear and trembling. For it is God which worketh in you both to will and to do of his good pleasure" (Phil. 2:12–13). We are indeed called to work out our salvation, but we do so because God works in us both the willing and doing, for even the most holy saint will never be more than a justified sinner before God in the imputed righteousness of Christ.

The relation of the promise of obedience to our struggle against sin is obvious: God has promised that He will work the obedience in us which He demands of us. It is part of the covenant He has made with us. It is a necessary consequence of the indwelling of the Spirit of holiness and a necessary fruit of the Spirit's uniting us to Christ's person and work. Therefore, the Lord will work is us that righteousness (Deut. 30:8) with which He has made us acceptable before Him (Deut. 30:6; Phil. 3:9), bringing us into conformity with who we are positionally (Titus 2:11–14; 3:8; Eph. 2:8–10). Let us then look not to ourselves for obedience, but to the Lord, believing His promise and calling on Him to work in us what will please Him.

God Promises Us Repentance
God promises faith in Christ to all whom He has chosen to save; He promises us a certain and unshakable hope in His full performance of His Word, especially regarding our redemption; He promises us obedience to all that He commands of us. But what of our many failings? We

learned in the previous chapter that He promises to have mercy on us, to pardon our sin, and to restore us to usefulness. But what has God promised us regarding our failings? The Lord has promised repentance, and with it, confession of sin, mourning for sin, mortifying of sin, and turning from sin.

Like faith, repentance is a grace of God freely offered in the gospel and graciously worked in all whom the Lord chooses to call to Himself in salvation. Speaking of the resurrected Jesus, Peter said, "Him hath God exalted with his right hand to be a Prince and a Saviour, for to give repentance to Israel, and forgiveness of sins" (Acts 5:31). In Luke 24:47, Jesus declares that it was written of old that "repentance and remission of sins should be preached in his name among all nations, beginning at Jerusalem." When the apostles heard Peter's report of his visit to the house of Cornelius, they "glorified God, saying, Then hath God also to the Gentiles granted repentance unto life" (Acts 11:18). Therefore, as the Lord has promised faith, so He has promised repentance, for to believe on the Lord Jesus Christ for salvation begins with forsaking or repenting all other idols (1 Thess. 1:9). Faith and repentance are distinct but inseparable works that God accomplishes in us by uniting us to Christ in salvation by His Spirit. But this repentance has several distinct parts.

First, God has promised confession of our sin. That beloved verse of John that promises forgiveness and cleansing (1 John 1:9) is conditioned on confession. The same thing is seen in Psalm 32:5: "I said, I will confess my transgressions unto the Lord, and thou forgavest the iniquity of my sin." If forgiveness is freely promised in the covenant, though conditioned on a confession that we cannot squeeze out of our own hearts, then such a condition must also be freely promised (Deut. 30:6–8).

Second, God has promised mourning for our sin. To effect this grace, God promises to remove the hardness of our hearts regarding sin and to replace it with a softness and tenderness by which we tremble at God's judgments and grieve over our sin. The promise of such mourning is expressed in Zechariah 12:10: "And I will pour upon the house of David, and upon the inhabitants of Jerusalem, the spirit of grace and of supplications: and they shall look upon me whom they have pierced, and they shall mourn for him, as one mourneth for his only son, and shall be in bitterness for him, as one that is in bitterness for his first-born." In Ezekiel 20, God promises to restore His idolatrous people to Himself and promises that they will mourn for their sin. Verse 43 says, "And there shall ye remember your ways, and all your doings, wherein ye have been defiled; and ye shall loathe yourselves in your own sight for all your evils that ye have committed."

Third, the Lord promises mortifying of our sin. This grace is promised in Galatians 5:16, where the Lord says His Spirit strives against our sin, which results in the fruits of His Spirit blossoming in our lives (Gal. 5:22–25). This grace is also promised in Titus 2:14, which says Christ has redeemed us from all iniquity and makes us zealous for good works. In addition, in Romans 6:14, the apostle says, "For sin shall not have dominion over you: for ye are not under the law, but under grace." Though many consider this verse to be an imperative command, it is not. The verb is indicative, which means the apostle is indicating a fact which is, not which ought to be. Thus, for us who are united to Christ by saving faith, sin no longer has dominion. Just as the Lord promised to cleanse Israel from their idols, so the Lord will cleanse us from our particular sins by mortification.

Finally, the Lord promises turning from our sin unto Him. In Ezekiel 36:31, the Lord promises that His people will loathe themselves for their wicked ways. To loathe oneself because of wickedness is to turn from such iniquity and do it no more. Isaiah 10:21 says, "The remnant shall return…unto the mighty God" out of the captivity into which their sins have sent them. In Hosea 2, God promises to show mercy to Israel because of their great sin, which results in her turning to God by repentance: "Then shall she say, I will go and return to my first husband; for then was it better with me than now" (v. 7). When God promises Jeremiah that He will remember the exiles He sent out of Judah, He makes this promise: "I will give them an heart to know me, that I am the LORD: and they shall be my people, and I will be their God: for they shall return unto me with their whole heart" (Jer. 24:7).

The relationship of God's promise of repentance to our struggle against sin is this: God promises that we will overcome sin and be conformed to the image of Christ. This promise is part of His covenant and a necessary part of the promise of faith and obedience, all of which belong to the promise to purge us of sin and sanctify us for His glory. He will not leave us in our sin but will increasingly bring us out of it. He will not permit us to be overcome by sin but will overcome it in us for the sake of Christ His Son, who purchased us for His glory. Peter says this is the advantage that flows to a Christian out of the promises. By the promises we are made "partakers of the divine nature, having escaped the corruption that is in the world through lust" (2 Peter 1:4).

As we reflect on the promises of sanctification that the Lord makes to us in our ongoing struggle against sin, we must never forget that our righteousness is in Christ and not in ourselves. Ours is the faith, the empty and passive hand by which we receive God's gifts, but Christ's is the righteousness that justifies and upon which the whole sanctifying process rests. As we strive to obey God's commandments and are daily confronted with our failures, we must remember that the perfection of sincerity is ours while the perfection of duty is Christ's. Ours is the striving as an outflow of our gratitude for our salvation, while Christ's is the presenting of an abiding and perfect righteousness before God on our behalf. Our holiness is the fruit of which His is the root. We ever stand in Him and therefore rest our assurance of salvation not on anything we see in us, which will ever be partial and imperfect, but on His righteousness, which has been graciously imputed to us and which we have received by faith alone. Glory be to God alone!

Applications in Our Struggle Against Sin

Here is a summary of the major thoughts that apply to our struggle against sin that the Puritans provide us:

1. Take the greatest comfort from your union with Christ, for this flower is more full of holy nectar than you will ever be able to draw out. Consider it everything that you are united to Christ, that you are in Him, and that you are hid with Christ in God, for Christ will

not suffer any to perish who are engrafted into Him (John 6:37–40; 17:22–26).[19]

2. When you feel discouraged by the little strength you have to master your besetting corruptions, apply to yourself those promises in which the Lord Himself undertakes the work. For example, take refuge in the promise of Micah 7:19, "He will subdue our iniquities," and that of Isaiah 1:25, "And I will turn my hand upon thee, and purely purge away thy dross."[20] What the Lord has promised to do, He will surely perform.

3. If a strong and importunate lust is so natural and habitual to you that you despair of ever being able to conquer it, remember that God has promised to break the dominion of every sin.[21] Not a single sin in your life can challenge Romans 6:6, "Our old man is crucified with him, that the body of sin might be destroyed, that henceforth we should not serve sin," or Galatians 5:24, "And they that are Christ's have crucified the flesh with the affections and lusts." Do you believe this? You must! Therefore, challenge every sin, especially a besetting sin, with God's words of truth.

4. Can you have a better promise of the Lord's working in you to sanctify you than 1 Thessalonians 5:23–24? "And the very God of peace sanctify you wholly; and I pray God your whole spirit and soul and body be preserved blameless unto the coming of our Lord Jesus Christ. Faithful is he that calleth you, *who also will do it.*"[22] You must believe as confidently as the old man whom Leigh references: "An old man being once asked if he grew in goodness, said, yes doubtless, I believe it to be so, for God has said it!"[23]

5. When you feel stagnant and spiritually dry, as though you are not growing in grace, recall the Lord's promise that He will grow you and increase your grace, not by drops or sprinkles, but by pouring it out in abundance (Isa. 44:3–4).[24]

---

19. Leigh, 226.
20. Ibid., 328–29.
21. Ibid., 329.
22. Emphasis added.
23. Leigh, 343.
24. Ibid.

6. Look not to yourself to bring forth fruits of repentance, but to the Lord, for He promises to make you fruitful. "He is compared to a husbandman, the Church to an orchard, [and] the faithful to young plants, whose nature is to spread, and shoot out their branches, and bring forth fruit, John 15:2."[25]

7. As you look to Christ to make you fruitful, look to the Spirit, for until He quickens you and by His power fashions you unto holiness, you are just a lifeless lump of unformed clay. Without His continual breathings upon you, you are disjointed and weak members who have neither constancy nor uniformity in your motions or actions.[26]

8. Take special care, as the apostle says, to "quench not the Spirit" (1 Thess. 5:19). Do not provoke Him by your sin to stand afar off, for He is the fountain of your grace for holiness. He must quicken, excite, and apply your new life unto particular duties of obedience, but you must maintain close communion with Him.[27]

9. If you grieve the Holy Spirit by your careless demeanor toward Him, not a single promise can make you glad. If you provoke Him to withdraw and suspend His light, no rays from the promises can free you from the darkness of His desertion. If you make Him your enemy by purposely ignoring His conviction, none of the promises can speak peace to you.[28]

10. When you struggle with a strong lust and feel defeated by its incessant blows, go to the Lord and plead the covenant. Say, "Lord, I feel this temptation is too strong for me and is a lust I cannot overcome; as Thou hast said that Thou wilt circumcise my heart, that Thou wilt dissolve these lusts and cleanse me of all idols, I call upon Thee to fulfil Thy own promises."[29] "We must with boldness and reverence challenge the covenant of grace. There cannot be a more forcible argument in prayer than to plead God's covenant and the interest we have in him."[30]

---

25. Ibid.
26. Spurstowe, 101.
27. Ibid., 102.
28. Ibid., 104.
29. Leigh, 329.
30. Ibid., 111.

11. When you feel your heart divided between a desire to please God and a sinful desire for "stolen waters," pray with David that the Lord would unite your heart to fear His name (Ps. 86:11). Go to God and say: "Lord, my heart is out of order. I desire to do the good before me, but I also desire to put it off. Mend my heart, O Lord, for it is Thy bargain, Thy own covenant; do it, O Lord, for Thy name's sake."[31]

12. In 2 Corinthians 6:16–18, Paul says God will dwell among us as our God and make us His people. Then comes the obligation to which this promise binds us: "Having therefore these promises, dearly beloved, let us cleanse ourselves from all filthiness of the flesh and spirit, perfecting holiness in the fear of God." God's covenant obligates you to give your whole self to holiness. The strength and means by which you are to fulfill and accomplish the work of sanctification to which God calls you lie within God's promises. They are to you what Samson's locks were to him; if you cut yourself off from them by unbelief, your strength to mortify and put off sin will decay, and you will become as other men.[32]

13. If you truly hate sin, though it often arises within you, do not be discouraged, for your sanctification is an ongoing process that will not be complete until Christ comes in glory and delivers you from the body of this death (Rom. 7:24–25).[33]

14. Remember that Christ will not subdue your sins all at once, but will do it little by little as He subdued the Canaanites for His people (Deut. 7:22).[34]

15. Living out your holiness in Christ will not come wholesale, but will require daily choices: daily putting off specific vices and putting on specific virtues, daily saying no to sin and yes to the Spirit's leading and conviction. As the apostle said, you must die daily to sin (1 Cor. 15:31).

16. You must believe that you have died to sin (Rom. 6:2). Sin is crucified unto you and you to it (Gal. 6:14). Do you struggle with lust? You are

---

31. Cf. ibid., 112.
32. Gray, 158–59.
33. Leigh, 329.
34. Ibid.

dead to lust. Is it anger? You are dead to that anger. If the power of sin is the law (1 Cor. 15:56) and you are not under the law but under grace (Rom. 6:14), then do not yield your members to unrighteousness as though sin is still your master. You are alive to God in Christ Jesus and must therefore yield your members unto righteousness, as those whose Lord and Master is Jesus.

17. Study Romans 7:14–25 to know that your struggle with sin is not inconsistent with a state of grace but instead is irrefutable evidence of it. Only those alive to Christ struggle with the old man (Rom. 7:17) and only those indwelt by the Spirit of the living God feel the contrary striving of the flesh at the threshold of every spiritual duty (Rom. 7:21).

18. God has given you faith. You, then, must believe His promises that relate to your sanctification and overcoming of sin. Do not doubt that He has given you His Spirit and that He is at work renovating your heart, preparing you for glory (John 14:1–3, 16–17).

19. God has given you hope, causing you to be born again to a living hope (1 Peter 1:3). Therefore, do not despair over the slow pace at which you seem to be approaching heaven. The Lord will complete the work He began in you and will just as surely bring you home to Himself.

20. God has given you obedience. Therefore, you must live by obedience, refusing to sin and giving yourself wholly to your duty. Though it is true that your works do not effect a holiness before God, yet you must never forget that your endeavoring after holiness is how the Lord works His holiness in you (Phil. 2:12–13).

21. God has given you repentance. Thus, you must confess your sins and grieve over them. Grieve most, not over the sin itself, but over the One whom you have sinned against, namely, the Triune God who has saved you and never done you ill. As a believer, this makes your sins greater than those of a heathen. View your sins in their true colors when you confess them to God, acknowledging that your sins were not out of ignorance but against covenant and seal, and on that account were worse than the sins of pagans. They sin against creation, but you have sinned against covenant; theirs are fornication, yours, adultery. Only by putting your sin in its true light will you be

able to properly grieve for it and sorrow over it (2 Cor. 7:10). Also, since God has given you repentance, you must make every effort to turn from sin and mortify it by starving it of your consent. To feed your sin by assent is to strengthen its pull on you; to starve it by denial is to subdue it and weaken its pull.

22. God has given you His Spirit. By Him you live unto God and enjoy the fullness of Christ. Therefore, you are no longer indebted to the flesh but to Christ and His Spirit. You must now live by Him to put to death the sins of the body (Rom. 8:12–13), which means you must put on the Lord Jesus Christ by obedience and make no provision for your flesh's evil desires (Rom. 13:14). You are no longer dead in sin but are alive to God. Walk worthy, then, of the salvation you have received, "perfecting holiness in the fear of God" (2 Cor. 7:1).

Study Questions

1. How does Paul's struggle in fighting sin, recorded in Romans 7:14–25, comfort struggling believers? Does Paul's account of this holy war help you grow in grace? If so, how?

2. Read Ezekiel 36:25–38 and John 3:11–12. What does the Spirit's work of regeneration, His uniting of a sinner to Christ, and His indwelling in the soul mean to you? How have you learned the indispensability of the Spirit's work in your own soul?

3. Where in Scripture has God promised saving faith to all He intends to save? What then prevents you from trusting this promise? Why is faith essential in our war against sin?

4. What is saving hope? How does it differ from faith? In whom should our hope be grounded? Why are we prone to give up hope when God has promised to give believers the Spirit of hope?

5. Why is obedience so essential to the Christian faith (Rom. 6:12–13)? What does Paul mean by "obedience to the faith"

(Rom. 1:5)? What is the condition of Christians who are not daily praying and striving to run in the way of all God's commandments (Ps. 119:32)? What should they do?

6. List five texts that assert God promises His Holy Spirit to sanctify believers. How does a believer's sanctification rest on the work of Christ and union with Him by Spirit-worked faith? Is sanctification entirely the Spirit's work? What role does a believer play in his own sanctification?

7. How does Acts 5:31 prove that God promises repentance to sinners? If Christ gives repentance, what part do we exercise in our repentance?

8. How does Romans 6:14 "indicate a fact which is, not which ought to be" (p. 133)? How is this comforting? When we feel that sin has too great a role in our lives, how can this text be unsettling? What is the difference between *falling* into sin and *living* in sin?

9. We read, "As we strive to obey God's commandments and are daily confronted with our failures, we must remember that the perfection of sincerity is ours while the perfection of duty is Christ's" (p. 134). What is the difference between *perfection of sincerity* and the *perfection of duty*? How does this work out practically in daily life?

10. Read Romans 6:10. Why is it important for you as a believer to find your identity in Christ, thereby reckoning yourself dead to sin and alive to God in Christ? If you see yourself in this light, why is sin a foreign intruder?

Using God's Promises for Pursuing Holiness

Having considered the application of God's promises in times of affliction and temptation and in our struggle against sin, let us now consider how they should be applied in our pursuit of holiness. As the Lord has promised us strength to put off our old nature, so He has promised us strength to put on the new nature, "which after God is created in righteousness and true holiness" (Eph. 4:24).

One reason why Christians fail to grow in the grace and knowledge of Christ is that they fail to understand the relationship between putting off sin and putting on righteousness. It is generally accepted that all one needs to do to be more like Christ is to put off sin, but Paul repeatedly states that putting off sin must be accompanied by putting on righteousness. Consider the following passages: Romans 6:13 says, "Neither yield ye your members as instruments of unrighteousness unto sin: but yield yourselves unto God, as those that are alive from the dead, and your members as instruments of righteousness unto God." Romans 12:2 says, "And be not conformed to this world: but be ye transformed by the renewing of your mind, that ye may prove what is that good, and acceptable, and perfect, will of God." In Ephesians 5, Paul is more specific. He says, "Wherefore putting away lying, speak every man truth with his neighbor," then, "Let him that stole steal no more" (vv. 25, 28). He adds in Colossians 3: "But now ye also put off all these; anger, wrath, malice, blasphemy, filthy communication out of your mouth. Lie not one to another, seeing that ye have put off the old man with his deeds; and have put on the new man, which is renewed in knowledge after the image of him that created him" (vv. 8–10). Thus, putting off sin cannot be separated from putting on righteousness.

However, as we have noted, putting off sin or mortifying the flesh cannot be done in our own strength, but only in the strength of Christ working mortification in us by His Holy Spirit. The same must be said of putting on the new man, or what the Puritans called "vivification." We cannot put on righteousness in our own strength. We are helpless without Christ's Spirit, who alone vivifies us so that we might walk according to God's ways (Rom. 8:9–11). As the apostle says, "The evil which I would not, that I do, and the good that I would I do not" (Rom. 7:19). He also says, "I know that in me (in my flesh) dwelleth no good thing: for to will is present with me; but how to perform that which is good I find not" (Rom. 7:18). In other words, we are as powerless to do righteousness as we are to cease from unrighteousness. We cannot pursue either mortification or vivification without the work of the Spirit of God within us (John 15:4–5).

In addition, we are not to look to Christ for His blessing on our endeavors after righteousness. Rather, our trust is in His indwelling presence and power. Asking for Christ's blessing and help on our efforts is nothing more than depending on our own strength in hopes that He will come alongside and support it. That is not the pursuit of holiness "without which no man shall see the Lord" (Heb. 12:14), but the pursuit of a self-righteousness in which we dare not be found on the Judgment Day (Phil. 3:7–9).

To find true holiness, we must fix our eyes on Christ's indwelling presence and sanctifying power. We must say with Paul, "I am crucified with Christ: nevertheless I live; yet not I, but Christ liveth in me: and the life which I now live in the flesh I live by the faith of the Son of God" (Gal. 2:20). We must trust in the life-giving Spirit of Christ, who works in us the *willing* and *doing* of His good pleasure (Phil. 2:13). The fruits of holiness, which God looks for in us, are not those we manage to staple on and which fall to the ground with the first wind of worldly care (Mark 4:16–19). Rather, the true fruits of holiness are brought forth by the Holy Spirit of God, who sovereignly and effectually works through appointed means to enliven us in the way of righteousness and to help us increasingly die to self.

Our aim in this final chapter is to highlight some of the means by which the Spirit makes us alive to righteousness, for while we entirely depend on the Spirit for righteousness (Phil. 2:13; Rom. 8:4), it is still *our* doing. His is the cause and ours the effect, not the reverse. Thus, while we fully recognize that the Spirit is the origin of holiness, we also recognize our calling to "work out [our] own salvation with fear and trembling" (Phil. 2:12). We look to Christ to *enable* us to die to sin and live unto God (Rom. 6:4), to cease to do evil and learn to do well (Isa. 1:16–17), to lay aside every weight and run the Christian race with patience (Heb. 12:1).

How do we pursue holiness without self-reliance? How do we put on righteousness and live fruitful lives, not by our natural strength, but by the strength of Christ who indwells us? The answers to these questions are the powerful and effective means that God has divinely appointed *for* us and through which He promises to bless us *with* growth in grace and the lifelong pursuit of holiness.

In other words, a life of holiness—one in which we enjoy the fullness of our spiritual blessings in Christ and shine like lights to the glory of God in a dark world—is not the result of mere happenstance or even strong desire. Rather, it is the Spirit-born fruit of deliberate steps taken in pursuit of holiness. It is the result of diligently using the means appointed by God to bring about holiness. It is the outcome of a life of dedication and devotion to God. It is God's blessing on our concerted effort to grow in the grace and knowledge of Christ (2 Peter 3:18). Would you have the zeal of the apostle Paul, the faith of Abraham, the trust of Noah, the prayer life of David, the passion of Asaph, the fruitfulness of James, the resolve of Peter, the patience of Job, and the dedication of Elijah? Then offer yourselves without restraint to the duties appointed by God to bring about such a life!

Our Resistance to Spiritual Duties

In 2 Kings 5:1–14, we read about Naaman, the commander of the army of the king of Syria, who was afflicted with leprosy. His wife's servant girl told Naaman that a prophet in Samaria could cure him, so he travelled a long way to the home of Elisha, the man of God. Elisha sent a messenger to Naaman, telling him, "Wash in Jordan seven times, and thy flesh shall come again to thee, and thou shalt be clean" (v. 10). An easier means promising such incomparable results could not be imagined. Go, wash, and be healed!

But Naaman had expected that Elisha would offer a more dramatic means to cure an incurable disease, and when he did not, Naaman was angry (v. 11). Several rivers in his own country were better than the waters of Israel, he reasoned, so if he could be healed by dipping into a river seven times, he might as well go home and do it (v. 12). Naaman's servants stopped him, though, saying: "My father, if the prophet had bid thee do some great thing, wouldest thou not have done it? how much rather then, when he saith to thee, Wash, and be clean?" (v. 13). Naaman saw the truth in their words and obeyed the prophet. Verse 14 tells us he "dipped himself seven times in Jordan, according to the saying of the man of God: and his flesh came again like unto the flesh of a little child, and he was clean."

How foolish Naaman must have felt for doubting the word of the man of God and being unwilling to submit to the simple command to wash himself in the Jordan. How thankful he must have felt after finding himself cured of leprosy!

We are much like Naaman regarding spiritual duties. God has appointed certain duties as means of grace whereby we can subdue and mortify our sin (Rom. 8:13) and proportionally receive the innumerable spiritual blessings that are ours in Christ (Eph. 1:3). These duties include such things as prayer, Bible reading, and participating in the ordinances of public worship, such as the ministry of the Word and sacraments and the fellowship of believers. Like Naaman, many people tend to minimize such things, deeming them a waste of time. They do not see how such simple practices will lead to the spiritual growth that they seek, so they search for the latest extraordinary means prescribed by popular spiritual gurus. Or they dip two or three times in the means of grace and, seeing no immediate results, give up.

Let us pray that this chapter will serve as Naaman's servants to every reader, urging all of us to put off our reluctance and obey those simple means appointed by God to bring about our holiness. Pray that we might believe that He who is our Governor is also our Benefactor, and that He appoints such duties for our eternal good. Pray that we might not judge God's appointed means to be unworthy of our efforts, believing that He who is gracious and mighty to promise holiness is also wise in appointing the means by which He brings it about. Pray that we might not prove ourselves insincere and double-minded by saying we long for holiness but are put off by the difficulty of the means.[1]

Pray that we might put off slothfulness, unbelief, and procrastination, and be diligent in using the means of grace. They are not a cistern or pool that offers stagnant, aged waters that might be drained from overuse; rather, they are fountains and springs from which God's sanctifying and maturing graces flow to us as living and healing waters. Oh, that we might drink to our heart's content and be washed white as snow! As the Lord Himself has appointed these means and promised to bless them, we must doubt neither His wisdom nor His faithfulness, but instead faithfully and zealously give ourselves unto them.

If we put off the means of grace, we will fare no better than Naaman prior to dipping in the Jordan, but if we give ourselves wholeheartedly and unreservedly to them, by God's grace we will fare as Naaman did after bathing seven times in the Jordan. God has inseparably connected the means and the end; leave off the means and the end cannot be, but attend to the means and the end cannot fail to be.

The Means of Prayer

Of all the spiritual duties God has appointed for our growth, we have the greatest difficulty with prayer. Strictly speaking, praying is not difficult to master, for even a child can ask, seek, and knock. Praying is not difficult to do, either, for it can be done without hands, eyes, or even

---

1. We are indebted to *The Works of Thomas Manton* (repr., Birmingham, Ala.: Solid Ground Christian Books, 2008), 1: 378–79, for these pleas to reconcile our hearts to spiritual duties.

words. The place for prayer is not difficult to find, for prayer can be done anywhere. Neither is it difficult to find time for prayer, for a prayer can be as short as a single cry.

Indeed, the beauty of prayer is that we can give ourselves to it anywhere, anytime, and for any length of time. We can pray with our thoughts as well as our words; we can pray while engaging with others as well as in a moment of solitude. When we cannot be at church, we can still pray. When we are hindered from reading, we can still pray. When the public means of grace are denied us, we can still pray. When our eyes, hands, legs, and even our words fail us, we can still pray. There is no unfit season or place for heartfelt prayer to God. It should not surprise us, then, that no spiritual duty promises as much profit as prayer. Indeed, God has attached the most promises to prayer. He promises to turn our hearts toward prayer, to help us pray, to hear our prayers, to answer our prayers, and to grow us in grace in prayer.

By virtue of our old nature, which hangs on us like a scab, we are inclined to reject all the means of grace, but none so much as prayer. We hardly begin to pray and we are ready to be done. Though we know we should pray and very much feel the need for prayer, we put it off time and again until at last our eyes are heavy with sleep and we find ourselves unable to pray. No excuses come to us more easily than those that keep us from prayer. Yet God's promises to turn our hearts toward prayer are an inestimable comfort.

We have an unshakable promise of this grace in Psalm 10:17: "LORD, thou hast heard the desire of the humble: thou wilt prepare their heart, thou wilt cause thine ear to hear." God prepares our hearts for prayer by placing His desires within us. We are not bent toward prayer because we are plagued by sinful desires that run contrary to our spiritual desires. Thus, though we want to pray, we also do not want to pray (Rom. 7:21–23). We need a divine hand to incline our hearts toward prayer, which is the very thing promised in this verse and supported by the apostle in Romans 8:26: "The Spirit also helpeth our infirmities: for we know not what we should pray for as we ought." The Spirit, who indwells us, places right desires within our hearts, then moves us to voice those desires to God in prayer, for without Him, we neither know how to pray nor rightly desire to pray.

We know that the godly call upon God because the Spirit graciously moves them to it. It is by our prayers that God has chosen to bring about His eternal decree. In Ezekiel 36, God promises redemption for His people, not for their sakes, but for the sake of His name, which He has sovereignly and covenantally placed upon them (Ex. 34:5–7). But the Lord closes this prophecy by saying in verse 37, "I will yet for this be inquired of by the house of Israel, to do it for them." In other words, though God has sovereignly promised to redeem His people, He also places the desire for redemption within their hearts and turns them toward prayer for it. His decree is not conditioned on man's desire and prayers, but His decree includes man's desire and prayers as the appointed means to the appointed end. Oh, that we would believe this promise, which has its roots in God's eternal decree, and look for more Spirit than speech in our prayers![2] As it is impossible that God's decree should fail, so it is impossible that any part of it will fail, including the gracious moving of our hearts toward prayer.

It is not enough to be inclined toward prayer; we must actually pray. We need the Spirit's help to put these holy desires into action. Part of the Holy Spirit's ministry is to help us approach the throne of God as we ought, and to give voice to the desires that He has placed within us as the means to draw us nearer to God and bring about God's will for our lives (Rom. 8:27). This spiritual work is affirmed in Zechariah 12:10, which says, "I will pour upon the house of David, and upon the inhabitants of Jerusalem, the spirit of grace and of supplications." Given the teaching of these two verses, Edward Leigh says that as soon as the Spirit of grace enters into the heart of a person, He stirs it unto plentiful and abundant supplicating and suing God for grace and mercy.[3]

God has also bound Himself by many promises to hear us when we call on Him. Zechariah 13:9 says, "They shall call on my name, and I will hear them." After Solomon's prayer of dedication, the Lord made this promise to him: "Now mine eyes shall be open, and mine ears attend

---

2. Leigh, 349.
3. Ibid.

unto the prayer that is made in this place" (2 Chron. 7:15). Proverbs 15 teaches us that God hears the prayer of the righteous because they are a delight to Him (vv. 8, 29). David was so assured of God's attentiveness to his prayers that he called Him by that name in Psalm 65:2: "O thou that hearest prayer." Could we have greater encouragement than this? David's words assure us beyond doubt that our God hears us when we cry unto Him: "I sought the LORD, and he heard me.... This poor man cried, and the LORD heard him.... The eyes of the LORD are upon the righteous, and his ears are open to their cry.... The righteous cry, and the LORD heareth" (Ps. 34:4, 6, 15, 17).

God hears our prayers and He also promises to answer our prayers in accordance with His glory and our eternal good. Zechariah 13:9 says, "They shall call on my name, and I will hear them: I will say, it is my people: and they shall say, the LORD is my God." Our prayers stir the Lord to answer us; His ears are open so that His hands might not be idle. Look again at Psalm 34 and notice what happens after God hears prayer: "I sought the LORD, and he heard me, *and delivered me from all my fears*.... This poor man cried, and the LORD heard him, *and saved him out of all his troubles*.... The righteous cry, and the LORD heareth, *and delivereth them out of all their troubles*" (Ps. 34:4, 6, 17, emphasis added). If we had no other promise that the Lord will answer us, His own words would be enough: "And I say unto you, Ask, and it shall be given you; seek, and ye shall find; knock, and it shall be opened unto you" (Luke 11:9). The Lord's answers are guided by His good, acceptable, and perfect will: "And this is the confidence that we have in him, that, if we ask any thing according to his will, he heareth us: And if we know that he hear us, whatsoever we ask, we know that we have the petitions that we desired of him" (1 John 5:14–15).

Finally, God promises that prayer is a powerful means to bring about that holiness "without which no man shall see the Lord" (Heb. 12:14). This promise is clearly stated in Luke 11:13: "If ye then, being evil, know how to give good gifts unto your children: how much more shall your heavenly Father give the Holy Spirit to them that ask him?" God gives us His Spirit, the One who is the source of all spiritual blessings, the seal of those very blessings, the down payment and the first fruits of our eternal and unshakable inheritance in glory. Surely, then, we might ask for no other fruit of our prayers than more of the Spirit of holiness, who alone can sanctify, cleanse, and wash us so He might present us to Christ as a glorious church, without spot or wrinkle, holy and without blemish (Eph. 5:26–27). May God turn our hearts to prayer with diligence fit for those who are being prepared for eternity with Him (Heb. 12:14).

The Means of Reading Scripture

God has also appointed the reading of His Word as a means of grace. That is because the Scriptures of the Old and New Testaments, though written by appointed men, are entirely inspired by God. They were breathed out by Him through His chosen instruments (2 Peter 1:20–21) and are therefore God's very words (2 Tim. 3:16). Thus the Word is not a dead letter but the living Word of God (Heb. 4:12). The reading of Scripture, unlike all other books, allows us to listen to God's voice as if He stands before us in the flesh and speaks the very words written on its pages.

So the Scriptures are more than a great book. They are by definition "profitable for doctrine, for reproof, for correction, for instruction in righteousness: that the man of God may be perfect, thoroughly furnished unto all good works" (2 Tim. 3:16–17). To read the Word of God aright is to look upon a divine compass that always points north toward holiness and to partake of a divine cordial that causes both the purging of our sin and our healing unto holiness.

Yet how shamefully illiterate we are of this book! How few of us have ever read it cover to cover! Fewer still are in the habit of reading through it once a year. Just as we cannot physically grow without physical nourishment, so we cannot spiritually grow without the nourishment of God's Word. We neglect the regular reading of God's Word to our own detriment. May God therefore encourage us to be diligent with this means of grace, for He promises to help us understand His Word so it will profit us in all circumstances, and He promises to bless our reading of it so we may become holy.

What Peter says of Paul's letters can be said of the Scriptures as a whole: "some things are hard to be understood" (2 Peter 3:16). It may take many years of biblical instruction and many times of reading through the Bible before we can fully understand and appreciate the significance of a book like Leviticus or Philemon, or can adopt a position regarding the end times with any degree of certainty. Not all things in Scripture are equally plain to all. That is the Lord's way of keeping us humble. No one fully and clearly understands everything, and being reminded that God's thoughts are far above our thoughts helps us see that His Word is an inexhaustible well of heavenly wisdom. However, since God wills that we might be drawn to Christ with a childlike faith, all things necessary to salvation are indeed perspicuous and plain to all in God's Word.

As we grow in the grace and knowledge of Christ, we look to the Lord to help us understand His Word. Paul's direction to Timothy must be our approach to Scripture: "Consider what I say; and the Lord give thee understanding in all things" (2 Tim. 2:7). We are called to be faithful in our reading, and when we do not understand Scripture as we would like, we must look to the Lord and call upon His promises. Revelation 1:3 promises that those who read will be given understanding: "Blessed is he that readeth, and they that hear the words of this prophecy, and keep those things which are written therein: for the time is at hand." Proverbs 1:23 also promises the Lord will grant understanding of His instruction to all who turn to Him, saying, "Turn you at my reproof: behold, I will pour out my spirit unto you, I will make known my words unto you." And Psalm 19:7–8 teaches us that the purpose of the Word of God is not to confuse but to teach and instruct, to enlighten and make wise: "The testimony of the LORD is sure, making wise the simple. The statutes of the LORD are right, rejoicing the heart: the commandment of the LORD is pure, enlightening the eyes."

When we struggle to understand a passage of Scripture, we should remember what Paul teaches us in 1 Corinthians 2, that the wisdom in the Word of God is not the wisdom of this world (v. 6) but a hidden wisdom that God has ordained for our glory (v. 7). Such wisdom cannot be understood by our natural capacity, but only by a spiritual capacity (v. 14), which is the blessing we enjoy as Christians. Paul says this wisdom of God is revealed to us by His Spirit (v. 10) and apportioned to us in just measure (vv. 12–14), according to our spiritual capacity. Therefore, we are guaranteed that the understanding we need will not be denied us: first, because the Spirit in us is the very Spirit of wisdom given "that we might know" (v. 12), and second, because we have the mind of Christ (v. 16).

The reading of Scripture is also a means of grace because God promises His Word is all-sufficient. No matter what our need, no matter what the plight in which we find ourselves, no matter what the challenge of dealing with unbelievers, no matter how low, destitute, and afflicted we may be, God's Word is sufficient to meet our need.

If we need guidance, God's Word is our compass. Psalm 119:9, 24, 105 assures us: "Wherewithal shall a young man cleanse his way? by taking heed thereto according to thy word…. Thy testimonies also are my delight and my counselors…. Thy word is a lamp unto my feet, and a light unto my path." If we need a preventative against sin, a fortress and shield against temptation, God's Word is our protection: "Thy word have I hid in mine heart, that I might not sin against thee…. I thought on my ways, and turned my feet unto thy testimonies…. I have refrained my feet from every evil way, that I might keep thy word" (Ps. 119:11, 59, 101). If we need help in our afflictions, a staff to lean upon, or a cordial to heal, God's Word is sufficient: "This is my comfort in my affliction: for thy word hath quickened me…. Unless thy law had been my delights, I should then have perished in mine affliction" (Ps. 119:50, 92). If we feel at our wit's end with no escape—even in our darkest hour and under the heaviest affliction—God's Word assures us: "I am afflicted very much: quicken me, O LORD, according unto thy word" (Ps. 119:107). If we have lost hope, God's Word offers it to us: "Remember the word unto thy servant, upon which thou hast caused me to hope" (Ps. 119:49). If we are tempted by a world bent on riches, God's Word satisfies us: "The law of thy mouth is better unto me than thousands of gold and silver…. I rejoice at thy word, as one that findeth great spoil" (Ps. 119:72, 162). If we feel befuddled by the relativism in our world, we are assured that God's Word stands forever true: "Thy word is true from the beginning: and every one of thy righteous judgments endureth for ever" (Ps. 119:160). If we face arguments from this world and need an answer, God's Word equips us: "Thou through thy commandments hast made me wiser than mine enemies: for they are ever with me. I have more understanding than all my teachers: for thy testimonies are my meditation…. The entrance of thy words giveth light; it giveth understanding unto the simple" (Ps. 119:98–99, 130). And if we feel anxious about the things of life, God's Word alone tells us, "Great peace have they which love thy law: and nothing shall offend them" (Ps. 119:165). Truly, God's Word is sufficient to meet all our needs, whatever they may be.

Finally, God promises that reading His Word is a means of bringing about our holiness. As 2 Timothy 3:16–17 says, "All scripture is given by inspiration of God, and is profitable for doctrine, for reproof, for correction, for instruction in righteousness: that the man of God may be perfect, thoroughly furnished unto all good works." First Peter 2:2 charges us, as newborn babes, to "desire the sincere milk of the word, that ye may grow thereby." And what John says in Revelation 1:3 is true of all Scripture reading: "Blessed is he that readeth, and they that hear the words of this prophecy."

Reading God's Word is like swallowing a divine medication for our growth in grace. It is a divinely appointed means for our maturation in Christlikeness. If it were not so, Paul would not have charged Timothy, "Till I come, give attendance to reading, to exhortation, to doctrine… continue in them: for in doing this thou shalt both save thyself, and them that hear thee" (1 Tim. 4:13, 16).

If reading God's Word is so important, we do ourselves immeasurable damage by neglecting this means of grace. May the Lord help us to devote ourselves to His Word with all our mind and all our heart.

The Means of Observing the Lord's Day

The Lord's Day, or the Christian Sabbath, is the one day in seven that God commands His people to set aside for Him. Neither work nor selfish or worldly pursuits are to be done on that day; they may not be sinful in and of themselves, but they are inappropriate on the Lord's

Day. However, the Lord does not want us to be idle; He commands that this day be devoted entirely to Him in the pursuit of public, family, and private worship. In other words, the Lord's command frees us from worldly engagements so we might enjoy the freedom of giving ourselves wholly and unreservedly to Him. To encourage us to be faithful in this means, God promises that if we honor His day, we will enjoy untold blessings all our days. Isaiah 58 tells us, "If thou turn away thy foot from the sabbath, from doing thy pleasure on my holy day; and call the sabbath a delight, the holy of the LORD, honourable; and shalt honour him, not doing thine own ways, nor finding thine own pleasure, nor speaking thine own words: Then shalt thou delight thyself in the LORD; and I will cause thee to ride upon the high places of the earth, and feed thee with the heritage of Jacob thy father: for the mouth of the LORD hath spoken it" (vv. 13–14). With such a promise, how can we refuse to honor the Lord in the faithful observance of His day?

We ought to give ourselves unreservedly to God every day, of course, but not every day allows us the opportunities that the Lord's Day does, for other days, by necessity, must be taken up with other activities, whether school, work, recreation, or relaxation. The commandment to devote one day wholly to the Lord also tells us to work the other six days. The opportunities and privileges attached to the Lord's Day, which make it so special and therefore a special means of grace, include the preaching of the Word, the administration of the sacraments, and the fellowship of His people in the sanctuary.

The converting and sanctifying power of the preached Word is indisputable in Paul's advice to Timothy and Titus, two young pastors appointed to preach the gospel. For example, the incomparable benefit of the preached Word can be seen in Paul's charge to Timothy, including the weighty account he will have to give before God regarding it: "I charge thee therefore before God, and the Lord Jesus Christ, who shall judge the quick and the dead at his appearing and his kingdom; Preach the word; be instant in season, out of season; reprove, rebuke, exhort with all longsuffering and doctrine" (2 Tim. 4:1–2). Timothy's faithfulness in preaching not only would prepare him to stand before God as one who must give an account (James 3:1; Heb. 13:17), but also would prepare his listeners to stand before God on that day; him, by his faithful preaching, them, by their faithful listening (James 1:22–25). And when Paul charges Titus to faithful preaching, he says it is the very means by which he should effectively exhort the flock to a life of good works (Titus 2 and 3).

Preaching is an effective means to holiness because it is the proclamation of God's authoritative, inerrant, infallible, and all-sufficient Word (Ex. 4:15). In preaching, God speaks to us, God's name is enforced as authoritative, and God's Spirit ministers to us. He who preaches may be a mere man, but as an ordained preacher he is an ambassador, a herald, and a messenger of the Lord of hosts (Jer. 3:15). Preaching is a means of converting our hearts and sanctifying our lives to prepare us to stand before God unashamed and holy in Jesus Christ.

What makes the Lord's Day special is preaching, by which God speaks from heaven to His people, comforting, convicting, and constraining them. This cannot be done the same way on the other six days of the week. It cannot be experienced by watching a televangelist or listening to a taped sermon at home. Preaching is an exclusive means of grace that God has appointed for His day for His people in His house. We cannot afford to neglect it, but must put forth the greatest diligence to attend it, for it is a great sin against God and against His generous provision to avoid sitting regularly under the faithful preaching of His Word.

In addition, God has established the administration of the sacraments of baptism and the Lord's Supper as special means of grace. These sacraments are seals of the covenant of grace (Rom. 4:11) that we enjoy in Christ, and therefore are signs of our participation in all the benefits of that covenant by faith (Gal. 3:27; 1 Cor. 10:16–17). Baptism is a distinguishing seal upon believing parents and their children, while the Lord's Supper is a nourishing seal by which believers feed on Christ in His death and resurrection. To put it another way, baptism signifies our being engrafted into Christ while the Lord's Supper signifies our communion with Christ.

Paul says our participation in the sacraments is a goad for good works and the very reason why sin must be put off. These seals obligate us to live united to Christ, which means we must be dead to sin and alive to righteousness as He is (Rom. 6:4–6; Col. 2:11–13). Union with Christ means we must live in the nourishment of His righteous and holy life (Col. 2:6–7; Rom. 7:4–6). To continue in sin or to neglect the pursuit of righteousness is to live contrary to the seals God has placed on us in the sacraments, which obligate us to a life of holiness. These ordinances are given by God to His church to be administered by His appointed ministers (1 Cor. 4:1) as visible means of grace to accompany the preaching of the Word. That's why we do not perform baptisms at home or administer the Lord's Supper around the coffee table. It is a great sin against God to neglect the sacraments since He has graciously appointed them for us and made them such an effective means for our sanctification.

Finally, God commands the fellowship of His people as a means of grace exclusive to His day. We may enjoy fellowship with God's people throughout the week, but God does something special in our gathering on the Sabbath in His house of worship. He appoints ministers to administer the Word and sacraments for our growth, which, in turn, leads to our encouraging one another to faithfulness in the things of God. Hebrews 10:24–25 says, "Let us consider one another to provoke unto love and to good works: not forsaking the assembling of ourselves together, as the manner of some is; but exhorting one another: and so much the more, as ye see the day approaching." The faithful ministry of God's Word and sacraments is such an important means of grace for us that the Lord commands us to not neglect assembling for public worship. Assembling together allows us to receive blessings from God as well as to encourage one another to walk with Christ.

Ultimately, it is God's presence with us as we gather together on the Lord's Day that makes the Lord's Day and His sacraments so effective for our growth. After Christ appointed baptism as a sacrament for the church in Matthew 28:19, He sealed it with a promise: "Lo, I am with you alway, even unto the end of the world." Also, in Revelation 1:13, John saw Christ dwelling among the seven candlesticks representing the seven churches (v. 20), or the church universal.

The very command to keep the Lord's Day holy and to gather in corporate worship is a pledge of God's sanctifying presence among His people. The preaching of the Word is the voice of God on earth, the

sacraments bring Christ to us and lift us by faith to Him, and the communion of the saints is the fruit of God's Spirit binding us together and
using us as blessings to one another. No wonder David spoke so highly
of the sanctuary, saying: "A day in thy courts is better than a thousand.
I had rather be a doorkeeper in the house of my God, than to dwell in
the tents of wickedness. For the LORD God is a sun and shield: the LORD
will give grace and glory: no good thing will he withhold from them
that walk uprightly" (Ps. 84:10–11). If God were to withdraw from His
house on His day, nothing would be left but a whitewashed sepulcher,
a name upon the door but emptiness within, the profession of life but
possession of death.

God uses such humble means as prayer, reading Scripture, and gathering together on the Sabbath to prepare His people to appear before
Him in glory. May we therefore prize these means of sanctification
because of Christ, who promises to wield them for our eternal good.

Promises That Prepare Us for Death

The shortness of our days, the certainty of death, and the length of eternity make it necessary to die well, the Puritans used to say. The best way
to obtain comfort in death, William Spurstowe says, is to be diligent in
our participation in the promises of God and to use all the means of
grace to make our calling and election sure.[4]

Spurstowe says the only way to ensure that we will die well, enjoying
the comfort of God's promises in death, is to live well in the application
of the promises and faithful use of the means of grace. These are God's
means to our holiness, with which we will not be ashamed or afraid to
die. The only comfortable death is that of a saint, for the saint has lived
his life walking in the ways of God and therefore has nothing to fear in
death. His sins are forgiven, the Judge is his Elder Brother and Friend,
and his eternal abode in God's kingdom has already been prepared for
him. Death will be the entrance to eternal life, of which he has had a
foretaste in his Christian days. No wonder Balaam said, "Let me die the

---

4. Spurstowe, 207.

death of the righteous, and let my last end be like his!" (Num. 23:10). According to Revelation 14:13, blessing in death rests only on those who are in the Lord: "And I heard a voice from heaven saying unto me, Write, Blessed are the dead which die in the Lord."

But to expect to die like a saint without living like a saint is foolish presumption. Spurstowe says to expect to die comfortably after failing to live a holy life is as vain as looking for stars on earth and trees in heaven; to waste the oil of grace and yet think to be anointed with the oil of gladness is the fruit of presumption, not of faith. When servants idle away the light their Master gives them to work by, they may well conclude that they must go to bed in the dark. Even so, when Christians neglect in life to work out their salvation with fear and trembling, it is no wonder that in the night of death they lack the light of comfort and have a dark exit out of the world.[5]

That God promises such comfort in death for His people is clear from many verses. Romans 8:38–39 assures us, "For I am persuaded, that neither death, nor life, nor angels, nor principalities, nor powers, nor things present, nor things to come, nor height, nor depth, nor any other creature, shall be able to separate us from the love of God, which is in Christ Jesus our Lord." The very sting of death, the curse of God's law for our sin, has been removed by Christ's atoning work. Forgiveness flowed out of Christ's death, so that "then shall be brought to pass the saying that is written, Death is swallowed up in victory. O death, where is thy sting? O grave, where is thy victory? The sting of death is sin; and the strength of sin is the law. But thanks be to God, which giveth us the victory through our Lord Jesus Christ" (1 Cor. 15:54–57). Thus, the death of saints in Christ is likened in Scripture to a sweet sleep. Of Stephen, the first Christian martyr, we read: "He kneeled down, and cried with a loud voice, Lord, lay not this sin to their charge. And when he had said this, he fell asleep" (Acts 7:60). Isaiah calls the grave a bed of rest: "He shall enter into peace: they shall rest in their beds, each one walking in his uprightness" (57:2).

---

5. Ibid., 208.

Death is our friend and gain, says Philippians 1:21. As such, we are not to fear it, for the Lord has delivered us both from death and the fear of it (Heb. 2:14). We are sure of an abiding hope in our death (Prov. 14:32) because we enjoy a present hope in Christ. Let us therefore give ourselves with all diligence to the means God has appointed to prepare us for death, judgment, and eternity. Without them, we are without hope, but with them we have nothing to fear and can be sure that, in death and before the judgment seat of Christ, we will have the holiness "without which no man shall see the Lord" (Heb. 12:14). Remember, if the means of grace are nothing less than an investment in eternity, then the lack of them is an eternal deficit. May God enable us, by His great and precious promises, to invest well!

Some Ways to Pursue Holiness

Here is a summary of some Puritan thoughts on various ways to pursue holiness:

1. Understand that the means of grace are appointed by God. They are ineffective in themselves but derive their efficacy for growth from God's Spirit. Notwithstanding, they cannot be neglected without much harm. For example, while a farmer prepares his soil, plants his seed, and cultivates plants, he depends on God to bless his labors with good rain and sunshine, and thereby to bring about a great harvest. However, if the farmer neglects to prepare, plant, and cultivate, the sun and rain alone will not bring him a harvest. In the same way, you must give yourself diligently to the means of grace to expect a harvest of righteousness, not as the fruit of your labors but as God's blessing on His appointed means.

2. Remember that though God has promised to make you holy, these promises do not exclude the means He has appointed to bring it about. Just as there are promises made *of* grace, so there are promises made *to* grace. For example, while you cannot by any natural capacity hear and believe the preached Word, God has commanded

that you should hear the preached Word, for it is the means by which He converts and comforts you.[6]

3. Although the means of grace cannot effect holiness by themselves, they are so necessary for it that no one can be converted or sanctified who neglects or refuses the use of those means by which God is pleased to dispense His free and undeserved grace.[7]

4. It is true that God works some things without means, thus manifesting His great, omnipotent power. But He has willed to work most things in relation to our conversion and progress toward holiness by the use of means. Thus, your neglect of those means not only brings harm to you but dishonors God.[8]

5. While the means of grace carry God's promise that they will be fruitful, the manner and season in which they bear fruit are subject to His infinite wisdom and glory. "The godly sometimes walk without comfort, because they put it from themselves, and God oftentimes causes his children to seek long before they find comfort," Leigh says. "But the ardent desire shall at length be satisfied. Remission of sins and peace of conscience are favors worth waiting for. We have not waited so many years in the means of grace for comfort, as God has waited for our conversion."[9]

6. He that does not endeavor to grow in holiness by starving the desires of the flesh and strengthening the graces of the Spirit by renewing acts of godliness can be rich in neither grace nor comfort (Rom. 13:14).[10]

7. When you resist any duty, the covenant should spur you on; you should remember that you have taken earnest money, as it were, from God in your baptism, promising that you will live for Him. Remember as well that you have often renewed that first pledge in the sacrament of the Lord's Supper, and therefore you may not flinch from your bargain.[11]

---

6. Ibid., 66–68.
7. Ibid., 68.
8. Ibid., 69.
9. Leigh, 372.
10. Spurstowe, 272.
11. Leigh, 113.

8. Comfort yourself that God will accept your services in Christ, not on the basis of their perfection but their sincerity (Rom. 12:1; 1 Peter 2:5).

9. Believe the Word of the Lord that your labor in spiritual duties is not in vain but will bring about a harvest of righteousness, both in this life and the life to come (Gal. 6:9; 1 Cor. 15:58; James 1:12).[12]

10. Remember that each duty that God requires of you has been converted into a promise. Consider: faith is a duty (1 John 3:23) and a promise (Zech. 13:9); mortification is a duty (Col. 3:5) and a promise (Mic. 7:19); fear is a duty (Eccl. 12:13) and a promise (Jer. 32:40). Be assured that, by the grace of God, you are enabled to perform your duties unto God. When you are unable to do so, plead with Him to accomplish His promise in you to be faithful to His promise and exalt Himself by His omnipotence in causing you to obey Him in all things (Ezek. 36:27).[13]

11. As God has promised to help you in your duties, you must not look so much to the commandments that obligate you as to the promises that sustain you in your duties.[14]

12. Never forget this powerful truth: "God's promises are the foundation of all our performances; for we by working do not cause him to fulfill his promises, but he by promising doth enable us to perform our works."[15]

13. As you pursue holiness, return again and again to these promises: "And the very God of peace sanctify you wholly; and I pray God your whole spirit and soul and body be preserved blameless unto the coming of our Lord Jesus Christ. Faithful is he that calleth you, who also will do it" (1 Thess. 5:23–24) and "Now unto him that is able to keep you from falling, and to present you faultless before the presence of his glory with exceeding joy, to the only wise God our Saviour, be glory and majesty, dominion and power, both now and

---

12. Ibid., 346–47.
13. Gray, 119.
14. Leigh, 345.
15. Ibid., 346.

ever. Amen" (Jude 24–25). If the Lord is sanctifying you, He will surely complete His work.

14. When you struggle with prayer, take God's promises with you as you approach the throne. Having a promise in hand will help you pray with faith as you plead with God on the basis of His own Word; it will help you pray with an expectant heart and an open eye on the horizon of God's providence; it will keep you humble as you see that all you enjoy is the fruit of God's gracious promises; it will help you pray with love as you see the abundance of God's grace toward you; and it will help you pray with fervency as you plead for what God has already promised to give.[16]

15. Assure yourself as you pray that "God is more ready to hear, than we to ask; to give, than we to receive" (1 Peter 3:12).[17]

16. Remind yourself that "His ears are open, as a kind mother or nurse, which [is used to being] wakeful, that she will hear the child so soon as ever it begins to cry" (cf. Dan. 10:12; Isa. 65:24).[18]

17. Remember that God has assured you that your time of trouble is His set time of audience. By presenting Himself as the Lord whose ears are attentive to your prayers (1 Peter 3:12), He declares that His ear is leaned toward you. He hears every cry or sigh that you utter.[19]

18. In praying, ask, seek, and knock. "It is not a simple repetition of the same thing, but a gradation. *Ask* as a beggar, *Seek* as with a candle, *Knock* as one that hath power, with importunity."[20]

19. *Ask* with the mouth, *seek* with the heart, and *knock* with the hand, for "the Lord will give you temporal things, you shall find spiritual things, and eternal things shall be opened up unto you."[21]

20. Never forget that God will answer your prayers on the grounds of His covenant (Zech. 13:9). By grace, God will give, give, and never

16. Gray, 159–60.
17. Leigh, 351.
18. Ibid.
19. Ibid.
20. Ibid., 354.
21. Ibid., 354–55.

leave off giving, for His covenant does not allow it. He has promised Himself to you, and He is the infinite, eternal God of bottomless and shoreless bounty; all that has been given to you in Christ is yours to enjoy for the asking!

21. Regarding the ordinances of the Lord's Day, meditate on these wise words: God's ordinances are channels and conduits designed for grace to run in, and to convey and dispense the precious blessing of a new and spiritual life to those upon whom He is pleased to bestow it. Those who contemptuously turn their backs on the preaching of the Word and other external means of grace will come to a sad and fruitless end.[22]

22. Weigh the truth established in Isaiah 58:13–14: the promise of delighting ourselves in the Lord is confined to or conditioned upon the duty of delighting in the holy exercise of rightly observing the Lord's Day.[23]

23. If you find yourself afraid when death is at your door, remember that you will not be judged according to how you fare at the instant of death, but according to the general course of your life. Therefore, you must not distrust God's mercy in death but look rather to the seals of His mercy that have rested upon all your life, calling you to faith and sanctifying you throughout the days of your pilgrimage.[24]

24. If death is upon you and you feel as though God has withdrawn His comfortable presence, consider that God is allowing you the opportunity to put forth strong faith in Him in the midst of weak feelings (2 Cor. 12:9–10) as a witness to others.[25]

25. Remember that the way you evaluate your spiritual estate should chiefly be grounded on how you have lived your life rather than how you fare at the time of your death.[26] Even the hypocrite may appear to die well, but that will have no influence on how he fares at the

---

22. Spurstowe, 70.
23. Leigh, 372.
24. Spurstowe, 215.
25. Ibid., 211.
26. Ibid., 214.

Judgment, which will be "according to that he hath done, whether it be good or bad" (2 Cor. 5:10).

26. Consider: "The promises are wells of salvation flowing with the waters of life, but yet the strong Christian that expects to be refreshed by them, must be at pains to draw water out of them (Isa. 12:3). They are full breasts of consolation, but yet the weak Christian who is as the newborn babe, or new-weaned lamb, must suck these breasts (Isa. 66:11), if he is to be satisfied."[27]

27. Let your thankfulness for the promises of God be expressed for others to see and hear. Tell of the mercy, salvation, and peace you have received. If you have tasted that the Lord is good, do as the birds, which, when they come upon a feast, chirp and invite their fellows. So tell the hungry soul about the satisfying and blessed food of the promises; tell the dejected what reviving cordials they are; tell the poor what enduring riches are in them; tell the broken and wounded what healing balms they are; and thus encourage them all to take hold of the promises by a hand of faith. Cripples who returned with health from the Pool of Bethesda would hang up their crutches on the trees and their rags on the hedges nearby to win credit and esteem to the waters. So you must honor the wells of salvation by making known the great things that God has done for you and by leaving in every place where you go some testimony of your thankfulness and of God's goodness (Ps. 66:16).[28]

Study Questions

1. What did the Puritans mean by mortification and vivification? How are these like two sides of a coin? Why do we need the Spirit's grace as much for vivification as we do for mortification?

2. How can we pursue holiness without falling into self-reliance?

3. With regard to spiritual duties, what are some parallels between us and Naaman in 2 Kings 5?

---

27. Ibid., 71.
28. Ibid., 272–73.

4. Why, of all spiritual disciplines, has God attached the most promises to prayer? Why are we prone to neglect prayer when God takes such delight in receiving it and has connected so many promises to it?

5. Are you reading and searching the Scriptures daily? What kind of reading plan are you using? Does your plan include reading the entire Bible at least once a year?

6. Read Isaiah 58:13–14. Why is observing the Lord's Day an important part of our pursuit of holiness? How could we glean more on the Lord's Day in our (1) public worship, including the preached Word, the sacraments, public prayer, and the communion of saints; (2) family worship, including godly conversation; and (3) private worship?

7. Dying and death are formidable. How can God's promises reduce the fears of believers as they face "the king of terrors"? How can death be a believer's friend? What is the best way to prepare for death?

8. How can other spiritual disciplines not covered in this book help you grow in grace, such as meditation, journaling, evangelizing, exercising stewardship, and reading edifying literature?

9. How do we harm our spiritual lives when we neglect the spiritual disciplines or means of grace that God has provided? How can we rectify that damage?

10. What has profited you the most from reading this book and answering the study questions? After studying the promises of God, what changes should you make in your life with the assistance of the Holy Spirit?

APPENDIX

A Table of Promises

which I have observed in reading over the Bible, as they
are dispersed in the several books of Scripture

— *Edward Leigh*

OLD TESTAMENT

Genesis
3:15
6:18
8:22
9:2, 9, 11, 13, 15, 16, 27
12:2, 3
13:15, 16, 17
16:10, 12
17:2, 4, 6, 7, 8, 16, 20,
   21
18:10, 14, 18
21:12, 13
22:17, 18
26:2, 3, 24
28:13, 14, 15
31:3
35:11, 12
46:3, 4
48:19, 21
49:10, 25
50:24

Exodus
3:12, 21
4:12
6:6, 7, 8
8:22
12:13, 23
14:13
15:26
19:5, 6
20:2, 6, 24

23:20, 22, 23, 25, 26, 27
28:38
29:45, 46
30:6
32:10, 13
33:2, 14, 19
34:6, 7, 24

Leviticus
1:4
18:5
20:24
25:13, 18, 19, 21
26:4–13, 42, 44, 45

Numbers
6:27
11:17
15:25, 26, 28
18:5
20:8
21:8
23:19, 21, 23
24:7, 9, 17
25:12, 13
32:22
35:34

Deuteronomy
2:25
3:2, 21, 22, 28
4:1, 10, 29, 30, 31, 40

5:10, 29, 33
6:2, 3, 18
7:6, 9, 12, 13, 14, 15, 16
8:1
9:3, 14
10:9
11:8, 9, 12, 14, 15, 21,
   23, 24, 25, 27, 31
12:7, 12, 18, 25, 28
13:11
14:2, 29
15:4, 6, 18
16:15, 20
18:15, 18
19:13
20:1, 4
21:8
22:7
23:14, 20
24:19
25:15
26:18, 19
28:1–14
29:9
30:3–10, 16, 20
31:6, 8, 23
32:9, 30
33:11, 29

Joshua
1:5, 7, 8, 9
6:17

97:10, 11
98:9
102:15–18, 20
103:3, 8–13, 17, 18
106:3
107:9, 36, 38
110:2, 3
111:5, 10
112:1–4, 6–9
113:7, 8, 9
115:9–11, 13
116:15
117:2
118:5
119:1, 2, 49, 71, 130, 165
121:3, 4, 5, 6, 7, 8
122:6
125:1, 2, 3
126:5, 6
127:3, 5
128:1–6
130:4, 8
132:11–19
135:4
137:8, 9
138:6, 7
140:12, 13
144:15
145:8, 9, 13, 18, 19, 20
146:5, 7, 8, 9
147:2, 3, 6, 11, 19
149:4

Proverbs
1:7, 23, 33
2:4, 5, 7, 8, 9, 11, 12, 21
3:2, 4, 10, 12, 13, 16–18, 22–26, 33–35
4:9, 8, 9, 13, 18, 22
6:22, 24
7:5
8:17–19, 21, 34, 35
9:8, 9, 10
10:2, 3, 4, 6, 7, 9, 16, 17, 22, 24, 27–30

11:2–6, 8, 9, 18–22, 26, 27, 28, 30, 31
12:3, 6, 7, 11, 13, 14, 19–22, 24, 27, 28
13:2, 4, 6, 13, 15, 18, 20, 21, 25
14:11, 22, 26, 34
15:6, 8, 16, 29, 33
16:3, 7, 8, 13, 20
17:2
18:10, 12, 20
19:16, 17, 23
20:7, 28
21:21
22:4, 5, 9, 15, 19
23:13, 14, 24
24:14, 25
27:18
28:10, 13, 14, 18–20, 23, 25–27
29:17, 18, 23, 25
30:5

Ecclesiastes
8:12
11:1

Isaiah
1:18, 19
2:2, 3, 4
3:10
4:2, 5, 6
6:13
7:14
9:3, 6, 7
10:10, 20
11:1, 2, 4, 6–10, 12, 13
12:3
14:1, 2, 3
17:2, 6, 7, 8
19:17, 22, 24
22:22, 23
24:13
25:4, 6, 8, 9
26:3, 9, 12
27:3, 5, 6, 8, 9

28:5, 12
29:8, 19, 23, 24
30:18–27, 29
31:7
32:1, 2, 3, 4, 17, 18
33:6, 16, 17, 19, 20, 21, 24
35:1, 2, 4ff.
37:31, 32
38:5, 6
40:1–5, 10, 11, 29, 31
41:10–14, 16–19, 25
42:1, 3, 4, 6, 7, 16
43:1–5, 25
44:3–5, 22
45:17, 24, 25
46:4, 10, 13
48:9, 17, 18, 19
49:6, 8, 9, 10, 12, 13, 15, 16, 22, 23, 25, 26
50:10
51:3, 4, 5, 6, 11, 12, 13
52:1, 6, 10, 12, 13
53:5, 11, 12
54:3, 4, 5, 7ff.
55:1, 3, 5, 7, 9, 13
56:2, 5–8
57:2, 13, 15, 16, 18, 19
58:8–15
59:19, 20, 21
60:2–9, 13–18, 19, 20, 21, 22
62:2–4, 11
63:9
64:4
65:1, 9, 13, 14, 16, 17ff.
66:2, 5, 11–14, 18–20, 22

Jeremiah
1:8, 19
3:1, 12, 15, 17, 18
4:1, 2, 14
6:3, 16
7:3, 7, 23
11:4, 5

NEW TESTAMENT

Matthew
1:21
3:12
5:3–13
6:4, 6, 14, 18, 30, 32, 33
7:7, 8, 11, 21, 24
8:11
9:13
10:19, 22, 30, 32, 39,
    40–42
11:6, 28, 29
12:18–21, 31, 32, 50
13:30, 41, 43, 49
15:24
16:18, 19, 25, 27
17:11, 20
18:4, 5, 10, 11, 14, 18,
    20
19:14, 17, 21, 28–30
20:4, 6, 7
21:21, 22, 43
23:12
24:13, 14, 22, 24, 30, 31,
    35, 46–47
25:21, 23, 29, 31–34,
    40, 46
26:13, 26, 28
28:20

Mark
1:8
2:17
3:28, 35
4:11, 25
8:35
9:1, 23, 31, 37, 41
10:14, 21, 29, 30, 31
11:23, 24, 25
13:13, 22, 26, 27, 31
16:16, 17, 18

Luke
1:13–17, 23, 34, 35, 50,
    53, 74–77, 79

2:10, 11, 26
3:5, 6, 16
4:18
5:32
6:20–23, 35, 37, 38,
    47, 48
7:23
8:10, 21, 50
9:24, 27, 48
10:16, 19, 28, 42
11:9, 10, 13, 28, 41
12:7, 8, 10, 12, 28, 30,
    31, 32, 33, 37, 38,
    43, 48
13:29, 30
14:11, 14
15:7, 10
16:9
17:33
18:7, 8, 14, 16, 22, 27,
    30, 33
19:10, 26
21:15, 18, 27, 28, 33
22:19, 28–30, 32
23:43

John
1:1, 16, 17, 29, 50
2:51
3:3, 15–18, 36
4:14, 23
5:20, 24, 25, 28, 29
6:27, 35, 37, 39, 40, 44,
    45, 47, 51, 54–58
7:17, 38
8:31, 32, 36, 51, 52
9:31
10:9, 10, 14, 16, 27,
    28, 29
11:25, 26
12:32, 46, 47
13:1, 17, 20, 32, 35
14:2, 3, 6, 12, 13, 14,
    16–21, 23, 26, 27

15:2, 5, 7, 8, 10, 11, 14,
    15, 26
16:7, 13–16, 20, 22–25
17:2, 3, 9, 11, 13, 15, 17,
    19, 20, 21, 22, 24, 26
20:23, 29, 31

Acts
1:5, 8, 11
2:17, 18, 21, 38, 39
3:19, 22, 25, 26
7:34, 37
9:16
10:35, 43
11:14, 16
13:26, 34, 38, 39
15:16
16:31
17:31
18:10
20:32

Romans
1:16, 17
2:6, 7, 10
3:24, 25
4:7, 8, 16, 25
5:19, 20
6:14, 23
8:1, 11, 13, 16–18, 26,
    28–35, 37–39
9:4, 12, 15, 26, 33
10:4, 5, 9–13
11:23–27, 29, 32
12:20
13:3, 4
14:17, 18
15:4, 12
16:10

1 Corinthians
1:8, 30
2:9
3:8, 14, 22

Selected Readings
on God's Promises

à Brakel, Wilhelmus. "The Life of Faith in Reference to the Promises." In *The Christian's Reasonable Service*. Vol. 2. Trans. Bartel Elshout. Ed. Joel R. Beeke. Grand Rapids: Reformation Heritage Books, 1999.

Alleine, Joseph. *The Precious Promises of the Gospel*. Morgan, Penn.: Soli Deo Gloria, 2000. (40 pp.) This booklet is extracted from Richard Alleine's *Heaven Opened*. It is one of the two chapters written by Joseph Alleine.

Mackenzie, Lachlan. "The Great and Precious Promises." In *The Happy Man: The Abiding Witness of Lachlan Mackenzie*, 56–71. Edinburgh: Banner of Truth Trust, 1960.

Martin, Hugh. "Precept, Promise, and Prayer: An Illustration of the Harmony between Divine Sovereignty and Human Agency." In *Christ For Us: Sermons of Hugh Martin*, 114–138. Edinburgh: Banner of Truth Trust, 1998.

Miller, Graham. *The Treasury of His Promises: 366 Daily Readings*. Edinburgh: Banner of Truth, 1986.

Owen, John. "The Steadfastness of the Promises, and the Sinfulness of Staggering." In *The Works of John Owen*. Vol. 8. Reprint, Edinburgh: Banner of Truth Trust, 1967.

Pink, A. W. "Scripture and the Promises." In *Profiting from the Word*. London: Banner of Truth Trust, 1970.

Piper, John. *Battling Unbelief: Defeating Sin with Superior Pleasure*. Colorado Springs: Multnomah Books, 2007.

Reynolds, Edward. "The Pollution of Sin and Use of the Promises." In *The Whole Works of the Right Rev. Edward Reynolds*. Vol. 1. Reprint, Ligonier, Penn.: Soli Deo Gloria Publications, 1992.

Shepard, Thomas. "The Saint's Jewel; Showing How to Apply the Promise." In *The Works of Thomas Shepard*. Vol. 1. Reprint, Ligonier, Penn.: Soli Deo Gloria Publications, 1991.

Sibbes, Richard. "Yea and Amen; or Precious Promises and Priveleges. Spiritually unfolded in their nature and use. Driving at the assurance and establishing of weak believers." In *The Works of Richard Sibbes*. Vol. 4. Reprint, Edinburgh: Banner of Truth Trust, 1991.

Spurgeon, C. H. *According to Promise: God's Promises to Every Christian*. Ross-shire, U.K.: Christian Focus Publications, 1997.

Spurgeon, C. H. *The Cheque Book of the Bank of Faith: Being Precious Promises Arranged for Daily Use, with Brief Experimental Comments*. Repr., Ross-shire, U.K.: Christian Focus, 2009.

Winslow, Octavius. "The Preciousness of the Divine Promises." In *The Precious Things of God*. Morgan, Penn.: Soli Deo Gloria Publications, 1994.